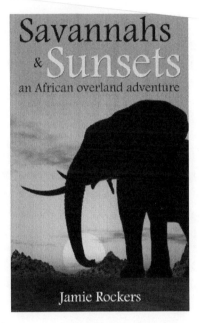

Savannahs & Sunsets

An African Overland Adventure

By Jamie Rockers

Savannahs & Sunsets

Copyright© Jamie Rockers 2013

Condition of Sale

ABOUT THE AUTHOR

Jamie Rockers is from Garnett, KS, USA and began her traveling "career" in Argentina in 2002. Since that time, she has studied in London and lived in Japan for four years, where she worked on a number of projects, including as a paid blogger on www.gaijinpot.com, followed by over 2 million people.

She has published six articles about traveling in Japan in *Japan Today*. She moved to Australia after backpacking through ten countries in Southeast Asia in the summer of 2010 and has currently relocated to the United Kingdom. She has travelled to over fifty different countries and lived in four, from learning to tango in Argentina to partying with sumo wrestlers in Japan to traveling across Russia by train.

Savannahs & Sunsets, An African Overland Adventure is her first published book. Another two will follow, one about her adventures through South East Asia and one about Argentina. Visit her website at www.jamierockers.com.

For my mother, who always thinks I'm far away

but who I always keep close in my heart.

"Twenty years from now you will be more disappointed by the things you didn't do than by the ones you did do. So throw off the bowlines, sail away from the safe harbor. Catch the trade winds in your sails. Explore. Dream. Discover."

—Mark Twain

Some names have been changed to protect privacy.

Table of Contents

Chapter One

"Into Africa"

Africa. What does that word conjure up in your imagination? For me, it is of vast savannahs in a sun-bleached land, of empty drifting dunes, soft sandy beaches with turquoise waters, an ancient and raw frontier where the skies are set aflame with the setting sun, and where the most exciting wildlife on earth coexist. I had always wanted to go to Africa. It is one of those places that I wrote in CAPS on my bucket list and somewhere I described as "ESSENTIAL TO TRAVEL TO". Although I have both traveled and lived abroad extensively, I always felt like Africa should be kept as the "final" destination in my traveling career. Not that I will never travel again, it just seems appropriate after trawling the globe, to leave Africa for last.

So after turning thirty, and realizing that there wasn't much time left before life's real responsibilities got in the way, I knew that it was time to go. So I gathered up my resources, suffered through eight vaccination shots against various deadly diseases, pinched my savings together, and took off on a three-month overland safari through Africa. Safari is a Swahili word that means "journey". Someone "on safari" was away and out of town, which summed up my trip perfectly.

Many people had asked me why I was going to Africa of all places, a continent that had seen horrible poverty and atrocities committed over the years. I wanted to see the Africa beyond what the newspapers and media said, the simple Africa that had nothing to do with war and poverty, child soldiers and corrupt politicians. I wanted to take a closer look at this continent and interpret it for myself.

I often wondered why people who wanted to travel didn't travel extensively more. Studies conducted with elderly people who are nearing death have shown that many of them wished they had travelled more. And not all the people who travel extensively do so because they are considered "lost".

In my own life, I have travelled and learned a lot and chose the life of unknown possibilities. And like the famous poem from Robert Frost about the fork in the road, it has made all the difference. Sometimes I think that we try to plan our lives out perfectly but we forget about luck. Luck happens to us all the time and whether or not we act upon those opportunities is up to us.

***

My first destination was Kenya. Upon arrival into Nairobi, the weather was *perfect*. It was sunny with dry heat and no humidity. It was heaven after being in England for so long (I'm American but currently living in England), with rainy and overcast days ruling my life for the past few months. From the window of my taxi from the airport, I watched scenes of Nairobi life; lean, ebony-skinned women with shaved heads dressed in long skirts with colorful African prints on them, some of them carrying bags of food on top of their heads; groups of smiling kids in school uniform walking to school, their hair braided in cool patterns, men dressed in long sleeve shirts and pants sitting along the side of the road in groups, chatting the day away. Lots of road workers stood about next to large holes in the earth just chatting. Strangely enough, it didn't really seem like anyone was working or at least, they weren't working hard.

Vendors with paintings, towels, potato chips, and ice cream wandered amongst the traffic when it stopped, gazing at drivers and passengers with hopeful eyes. *Matatus* lined the road, picking up people at random. *Matatus* were like mini-vans that carried a lot of people, most of whom sat on each other's laps. Being too close to someone else was just something you had to get over if you lived in Africa. The *matatu* drivers loved to get as many people as possible into their vans because, naturally, more people meant more money. Lots of big dump trucks carried dirt past us and the air was filled with choking dust. I pulled my blond hair into a tight knot and slipped on a pair of sunglasses as the wind blew through the cab and the sun shone down with intensity. I was excited to begin my journey. It was the start of a new adventure and I was feeling the newness of these foreign surroundings for the first time.

Some of the workers sitting along the side of the road stared at me with vague interest. I, of course, could not possibly go unnoticed here with my blond hair, green eyes, and pale skin, not to mention the huge backpack I was carrying on my petite frame. I was the foreigner here, the *mzungu*, which in Swahili meant "white person". The backpack was nearly the same size as I was and screamed out "tourist".

"Look sister," the taxi driver said, pointing to two giraffes grazing in an adjacent field separated by fence.

"*What?* I see them. Yes, two giraffes grazing!"

It was my first wild animal sighting in Africa and it had happened within thirty minutes of being in the country. And this was all after just coming from the airport. There was also a Maasai with his herd of goats in the large field.

"This land is government protected," the taxi driver explained.

The Maasai are a Nilotic ethnic group and are one of the many tribes in Kenya. They are semi-nomadic, and are perhaps the most famous of all the tribal groups in Africa due to their unique style of dress and their custom of drinking cow blood in their diet. The Tanzanian and Kenyan governments have instituted programs to encourage the Maasai to abandon their traditional semi-nomadic lifestyle, but the people have continued their age-old customs. I hope they weren't planning to abandon their customs anytime soon. Seeing them was like stepping back in time, a time that I could only imagine from looking at them. Because there are so many tribes in Kenya, many Kenyans consider their nationality to be of their tribal affiliation rather than of being 'Kenyan', which I found very interesting. Therefore, the Maasai would identify with being Maasai before Kenyan.

Kenya was a place where archaeological excavations around Lake Turkana in the 1970s had revealed skulls thought to be around two million years old and those of the earliest human beings ever discovered. What an exciting thing to think, that the first humans had potentially come from the very land that I was standing upon! Not to mention a land that played host to the annual wildebeest migration, which is the largest single movement of herd animals on the entire planet.

Nairobi, my jumping off point, had a population of 3 million people. The fact that its nickname was "Nai-robbery" did not comfort me. Violent crime and extreme poverty was a big problem of the city.

I was staying in the suburb of Karen, which was the wealthier suburb of Nairobi, in a place called Karen Camp. It was from here where I would depart on my overland adventure. Upon arrival, I checked into my dorm room and then decided to get something to eat. While I was perusing the menu at the bar for lunch, I chatted with an older white Kenyan guy.

"I like to come here for cheap beers," he exclaimed, making his point by slamming his bottle on the bar top and laughing.

He seemed a bit lonely and anxious to share his stories with someone.

"I had a real wild time growing up in Kenya," he reminisced. "I used to ride my motorbike really fast along the savannahs. But then I grew up and started to see all the problems that Kenya has, with the corrupt politicians. I think kids have it good, don't you think? They can live in their own peaceful and innocent worlds without knowing the real truth about the world."

I nodded, taking a sip of Tusker beer, the most popular Kenyan beer. I was disappointed that the bar didn't serve a local specialty of *nyama choma* (barbequed or roast meat). I had heard that you could buy the meat (usually goat) by the kilogram; it's then cooked over a charcoal pit and served in bite-sized pieces with a vegetable side dish.

Soon, a local Kenyan guy joined us by the name of Mr. Happy. Mr. Happy was very happy indeed, and I could see exactly how he had gotten his nickname.

"There are some strange rules that the Kenyan government enforce; no public smoking, no talking on cell phones in public, and a seriously crazy $4000 fine for loud noise," he explained. "These rules all have a reason though, as people have been hit by cars while chatting on cell phones, and clubs with loud music have opened next to schools."

Kenyans were conservative. I had noticed that women wore long skirts and covered their knees and shoulders when out. I could sense that even from looking at people on the street. The women were appropriately covered and there were signs for Christian churches everywhere. Religion, in the form of both Christianity and Islam, had a big presence in Kenya and this may have also contributed to the conservative way of thinking.

The bar began to fill with both expats and locals and it seemed to be a watering hole for the wealthier residents of Karen, most of whom appeared to be white. I suspected that many of these people had come from one of their fancy homes in the neighborhood, a home that was surrounded by high electric wire fence. Seeing these kinds of large houses with all their high security made me feel as though the gap between the rich and the poor might be considerably high in Nairobi. But it was just a guess. Mr. Happy told me that even in Karen, it wasn't safe to walk around alone. I hated labels and stereotyping of an entire city or nation and I am a firm believer that there are many more good people in the world than bad.

However, "Nai-robbery" didn't get its nickname for no reason. I planned to head Mr. Happy's advice. He was a local after all, and he certainly knew more than I did.

Chapter Two

"Scenes From Kenya"

"Goodbye Nairobi!" I yelled out the window of the overland truck.

I was leaving Nairobi and was officially on the road and lovin' it. The group of us on the truck came from all parts of the world and there were thirteen in total. Most of us were in our twenties or thirties. My overland trip through Africa had begun and I was at the beginning of a three-month vacation in Africa! What was there not to be excited about?

I honestly believe that travelling and experiencing another culture with an open mind makes people nicer. It also makes them question their own beliefs and see things from a new perspective. Not everyone does everything the same way. Are there right and wrong ways to do things? Maybe,

maybe not, but shouldn't you know all the options that exist out there before making up your mind that the way you do things is exactly right?

In my travels, I can instantly identify someone who is on a short trip and someone who is on a long trip. Someone who is on a short trip often talks about their own country a lot and how they do things there and makes a lot of contrasting suggestions between their home country and the country that they are visiting. Long term travelers stop doing that. They also stop asking where other travelers are from. Probably because they don't care but also because it doesn't really matter. What matters is engaging with other people and finding out what you have in common with them rather than how you are different from them.

I had to admit that I hadn't studied a lot about African history. Sure, I had done some research before the trip but that was another reason I was in Africa. To learn. For me, studying history and culture doesn't really stick strongly in my mind unless I visit the country or the place. Others may be different but it is still proven that *doing is learning*. Wanna learn about Roman history? Visit Rome and all the historical monuments! Want to learn about communism in Russia? Stay with a host family there and ask them about it. I've found that these are the things that stick in my mind and travelling and learning, along with meeting so many people from different cultures is what has made me feel comfortable around anyone from any background or culture. I can't stress the educational aspect of it enough.

I also didn't want to get to my death bed and think, "now why didn't I ever take that train journey through Europe or climb the Great Wall of China?

People tend to regret the things they didn't do, rather than the things that they did do. So, here I was, in Africa.

I gazed out the side of the truck. The sky was clear blue with a few fluffy white clouds. The dirt along the roads was an iron-rich red color and locals were walking along the road. If you were driving, you would have to consider both the road traffic, and the foot traffic of endless numbers of people walking along the side of the road. Road traffic seemed semi-organized, but people passed others at random and the roads were narrow. Some rode bicycles along the highway and I even saw one man on a bicycle grabbing a hold of the back of a semi-truck to pull him along. Now that was the way to catch a ride! Others took public transportation, which meant that there were around thirty people piled into one *matatu*, with some sitting on strangers' laps.

There were also a lot of people just lounging around at the side of the road, sitting beside it. Perhaps they were taking a break from walking. Many of them wore long-sleeved shirts and pants. It didn't seem that cold but there *was* a chill in the air and I wondered if this was what "cold" was in Kenya.

There weren't any modern buildings in any of the towns we passed, and all along the road, shanty towns linked up with each other. There seemed to be a market in every shanty town, where various stalls sold drinks, clothes, plastic bottles, etc. The markets looked dirty and there was trash everywhere. I was shocked by all the trash lying around, along the side of the road, in every yard, literally everywhere. People obviously didn't have a regard for the environment around them and were perhaps not properly educated and/or had the resources for recycling.

However, in all that chaos I could see there was a sense of community, where neighbors knew each other and everyone gathered together daily. Social ties were the glue here, the entertainment. After all, what else was there to do if there was no TV? This is what we had started to lose in the West, due to overconsumption of TV and busy life in general. I mean, I when is the last time you sat around chatting with your neighbor? I certainly hadn't for a very long time. Humans are social creatures by nature but in the business of modern everyday life, it has become easier to simply withdraw from this kind of community involvement.

Donkeys were everywhere, some of them skinny and pulling heavy carts of wood, others looking a bit healthier. Sheep, goats, cows, and donkeys all wandered through dirt parking lots and in fields. I wondered how people could tell which animals were theirs.

Locals waved at me from the road, mostly adults and a few kids. The kids who did wave were very excited and jumped up and down when they saw us pass by. Tiny shacks made from tin ruled the shanty towns and some of them had small patches of land for a garden. The garden held plots where corn and other veggies were planted, in what seemed like a rather haphazard pattern.

We arrived in the afternoon on our first official day of the trip to our camp near Nakuru National Park. When we arrived, we learned how to set up our tents. Over the next three months, 90% of my nights would be spent in a tent. I hadn't been camping that much and so it was definitely going to take some getting used to. I had outfitted myself with a head torch, sleeping bag, pillow, sleeping bag liner, and sleeping pad that was meant to go underneath the sleeping bag.

Unfortunately, that night as I shifted uncomfortably in my sleep, I realized that my sleeping pad was not meant for sleeping at all. It was meant for yoga. Perhaps I had overestimated my camping sensibilities.

Chapter Three

"Game Spotting"

It was time for game spotting. We were on our way to Nakuru National Park, the second most visited park in Africa. Our guide, Vincent, picked us up from the camp and we piled into an old white van that shook with every bump in the road. It definitely had no shocks and its frame seemed ready to crack. So it was a bone-jarring ride down twisting dirt roads to get to the main highway. I even felt my brain shaking as we bumped over all the potholes in the road.

On our way to the National Park, we passed motorcycles on the road piled high with firewood, logs, and crates. Cattle trucks rumbled down the potholed road, bumping along. People passed each other at random and once again, even at 6 A.M., the roads were full of women carrying large bags of rice on their head, young ladies wearing bright printed colorful skirts, kids on their way to school in school uniform, and men wearing clothes with NBA team logos and slacks. Some of the men even wore shirts that said, "University of Minnesota" or "Kansas City Chiefs", which was a shirt that was even hard to find in the US if you lived outside of Kansas, which was where I was from. They were clearly Salvation Army or other charity donations sent from abroad. I was glad to see that they were getting good use in Africa. Those shirts had been given a second life miles from the person who had originally owned them.

If there was one thing to say was that people around these parts woke up with the sunrise. The women amazed me with their balance. Some even carried buckets on top of their African headdress. And I am talking five-gallon bucket size here, not a tiny basket. Some women sat outside of run-down shops roasting ears of corn while others were busy stirring pots of what looked like stew that cooked over a small fire.

We reached Nakuru National Park and everything was covered in a thin wispy mist. Acacia trees, which are so famous in Africa, stood out of the mist like silent ghosts. Vincent and I chatted for a while about life in Kenya.

"I have never been out of my country and have hardly been out of this town," he explained. "I'm a tourist guide though, so I've taken tourists to national parks like the Serengeti and the Maasaii Mara."

The Maasai Mara had been set aside for the Maasai people to hunt, live in, and keep their traditions alive. The Serengeti and Maasai Mara were also top-class wildlife viewing spots.

"Many people don't have the money to travel for pleasure," Vincent explained. "I guess it is the same in Uganda, Tanzania, and Rwanda. I'm really grateful for my job because it helps me see more of my country. I am proud to be Kenyan and have no desire to visit other countries."

From a Western standpoint, this would have come out as sounding too prideful and perhaps, narrow-minded but I admired his sense of contentment, that he didn't need anything more or anything less. He was happy to be exactly where he was.

We headed into the mist of the park soon thereafter, along a twisting path lined with acacia trees and came to a beautiful and spooky-looking swamp, shrouded in thin fog. Trees rose out of the grey water and everything was silent, except for the occasional movement of a bird. Here, meat-eating storks lived among a variety of other birds. Someone in the safari van mentioned that they had seen a YouTube video of one of those storks just walking up to a pigeon and eating it whole. I guess sometimes it was a "bird eat bird" world, especially around these parts where the "circle of life" really did happen at an intense level. I usually wasn't really interested in bird watching (although I do like birds) but in Africa, where birds just ate each other whole, it was hard to not be interested in watching them to see if they might actually do it.

I stuck my head out of the open-top safari vehicle. Out of the ghostly mist, an African buffalo lingered near the trees. It had upturned horns that resembled a Viking helmet. It was absolutely huge. Another person in the van said they saw another video on YouTube that showed a buffalo and a rhino fighting and the rhino was tossing the buffalo up into the air. It was so big though, I couldn't imagine it being tossed about like a doll. But apparently there were bigger and badder beasts out there. I couldn't wait to see them.

We continued on, and out of the mist I spotted zebras and gazelles munching on grass side by side. The zebras looked like donkeys with stripes. Every zebra is different; the stripes differ, kind of like a fingerprint. They are a member of the horse family, but unlike horses or donkeys, they have never been domesticated. Some things were just not meant to be pets and zebras were one of them. The unique prints of the zebra sometimes made it difficult for lions to hunt them, because lions actually choose *who* in the pack they are going to hunt. If the zebra is running around with several others, it can easily blend in with its other striped friends and then the lion gets confused and soon loses track of its target. I liked zebras; they weren't dangerous and had cool stripes that even made them look almost make-believe sometimes. In fact, these animals were so strangely beautiful and unique, it seemed hard to believe that they were actually real.

I still couldn't believe that I was seeing these animals in the wild. It seemed surreal. It became even more surreal when further into this dream world of wild beasts and savannah, we came across a white rhino rolling in the mud. It was clearly enjoying itself, rolling over back and forth. In fact, we were so close to it, that at one point, it stood up and walked straight up to the van. It was nearly the same size. For a moment, I thought *we* were going to be the ones being flung into the air like a doll. The rhino was a highlight for most of us and even Vincent, the guide, said that it was rare to get so close.

Since we couldn't bear to tear ourselves away from the sight of the rhino, Vincent made that choice for us by driving off after a few minutes. We entered into a grove of shady trees and out of the woodwork came hundreds of baboons. From babies to elderly, all ages were represented. Some of them looked at us in curiosity while others continued to groom each other, picking out pieces of dirt or bugs from each other's hair. Alpha males threatened younger males who were overly confident and some of them swiped at each other. Babies rode on their mother's backs and clung to them helplessly.

We passed through the shady trees and into an open expanse, with hills rising in the distance, grasslands to our left, and a great stretch of lake on the right hand side. Because it was so early in the morning, the lake was very still and it was hard to tell where the water ended and the sky began, they were exactly the same steely blue color. Lining the edge of the soda lake were thousands of pink flamingoes, some of them perched on one long stick leg and gazing out to the lake. On the other side, a row of five zebras marched toward us as though they were in a parade. The acacia trees in the park, with their unique flat tops, held many birds in their thorny grasp. In fact the entire top of the acacia trees were covered in birds. A lonely buffalo stood near the flamingoes. His face was covered with mud from grazing on the wet grass. Perhaps he had lost his herd somewhere. Whatever had happened, he was at risk of being attacked by other carnivorous animals in this area as he was all alone. For these vegetarian animals, it was best to stick with the crowd.

We drove onward, up to the hills in the distance. We reached the top of one of them before long, and it offered a spectacular view. A thin layer of cloud covered the lake from this view but you could still see the shiny, steely blue water beneath it. An entire colony of hundreds of pink flamingoes rested by the shoreline, a sea of pale pink. The movements of the flock reminded me of the undulation of water, lapping at the shoreline.

We got out to look at the view. Vincent stood off to the side, chatting in Swahili on his cell phone. I wondered if he ever got bored of doing the same tour every day and explaining the same things day after day. As I looked out over the lake, I couldn't imagine ever getting bored of the view but then again, we always take for granted what is in our own backyards.

An hour later we were back at the bottom of the hill and passing two giraffes, which looked at us in surprise as we pulled up as close as we could to them. Once they had determined that we were not a threat, they began to pick and pull at a thorny acacia bush. They had long tongues that were covered in antiseptic and could somehow manage to eat the fruit on the branches, despite long thorns sticking out like daggers. I could now see that there were three of them, with their long necks sticking out from behind a tall bush. It was funny to see only the three necks and no bodies, it was almost like they were floating above the bush. Gazelle grazed nearby, always in a group. They looked so elegant and lovely. In addition to them, we spotted warthogs running around with their tail straight up in the air, as well as tiny jackals (which were no bigger than lapdogs, really). The variety of animal life on this small stretch of earth was incredible.

Further along, we stopped at a waterfall that ran with rich copper-colored muddy water. Some of the group wandered near the edge of the water but I held back. Who knew what was under that water? All I knew was that Africa was full of crocodiles.

After leaving the waterfall, we made our way to a safari lodge resort that was smack dab in the middle of the national park, on top of a large grassy hill. The resort was situated so that you could actually see wild animals grazing while you were sitting beside the pool. Here, you could let the animals come to you as it was clearly a top grazing spot. It was obviously very expensive to stay there and the people staying there didn't look like they would be too happy to sleep in a tent. The staff wasn't too friendly and when I tried to eat a banana that was in my handbag, even after I had ordered a drink, they told me that I couldn't eat it. And this was sitting beside the pool, not in a restaurant.

While I sipped my drink, I noticed a small grey monkey, with a black face and black feet and hands that made it look like he was wearing a black ski mask, black boots, and matching gloves. He ran around the lawn, drinking out of tea and coffee cups left behind by customers. At one point, he almost got his whole head stuck in a tea cup and couldn't get it off. Lucky for him, he managed to push it off just at the right time and scramble up a tree before the staff almost caught him. As he moved around, the staff chased him and threw sticks at him but he continued his antics. Someone went and grabbed a Maasai man out of nowhere to throw a monkey club at the monkey. Where he came from I have no idea, but he was dressed in his traditional clothing of a red plaid sarong with ankle bracelets and sandals made out of rubber. I closed my eyes in fear that he would hit the monkey and it would fall out of the tree dead. However, the monkey made a narrow escape onto the next roof. Lucky monkey.

Chapter Four

"The Long Road to Eldorat"

It would take two full days to get to Uganda. Our first night we would be staying in Eldorat, which wasn't too far from Nakuru, but because the roads were so bad, it was slow going, or *pole pole* in Swahili, which I kept hearing that meant "slowly, slowly". These two words seemed to symbolize the African philosophy. It could be said about almost anything. Why rush? There was nowhere anyone really had to be. If anything, Africa was the true test of patience.

Before setting out, we stopped for a couple of hours in Nakuru to run errands. As soon as I set foot in the local market, I was immediately surrounded by vendors, all vying for my attention with a variety of goods; animal-themed bookmarks, paintings depicting

Maasai life, post cards with giraffes, zebras, and elephants, and beautiful printed over-the-shoulder bags in a variety of designs and colors. My heartstrings were pulled when I was approached by a guy whose paintings were not so good, but who seemed desperate for me to buy one. Touching his arm, I offered my sincerest apologies. I couldn't buy from everyone, I really wished I could. I am the kind of person who has a high level of empathy for others and the vendors quickly find that they can break through my seemingly steely resolve in a heartbeat.

It was hard to explain to all the vendors that I was actually on a budget and couldn't spend the kind of money they wanted me to spend. It was hard to explain because to them, I had enough money to travel halfway around the world in the first place. So surely, I would have enough to buy a little something from just about everyone at the market. Although it hadn't been my intention, somehow I ended up with a painting of a zebra, along with several painted postcards, and a simple over-the-shoulder bag. With that, I finally managed to squeeze my way out of the market. At least I was buying from people who were selling; those who were working and not simply begging. The Kenyan government relied on Western aid in regards to their social welfare system. There were millions of dollars, pounds, and euros of aid going into Africa, into Kenya. Although it sounded cynical, I wondered when the Kenyan government would be able to implement and run their own social welfare system.

The guy who sold me the over-the-shoulder bag had originally wanted about 30 dollars for it but I ended up with it for around 8 dollars. It certainly wasn't worth 30 dollars, as nice as it was. It was more like an eco-bag. The vendor's friend told me his opinion on which over-the-shoulder bag looked best on me, while the vendor himself kept telling me he was a "gypo", a derogative term for gypsy in the U.K. I am assuming he thought I was British. I told him how much I was willing to spend on the bag and it didn't matter either way, but was up to him and I wasn't trying to cheat him out of any money. Even after I left the market, vendors continued to follow me down the road, begging me to buy more. I felt really sorry for them. Even after I got in the truck, the vendors were still outside the window trying to get me to buy things from them. But at this point, it just wasn't going to happen.

Escaping the vendors, we were soon back on the road and driving through the Nandi Hills, which were situated on the edge of the Rift Valley. The area was known for both its tea and its runners. Nandi Hills was called the "cradle of Kenyan running", and several long distance runners had hailed from these hills. Cows grazed upon the green highlands and rivers of golden corn dotted the landscape, the husks swishing in the wind. Laundry hung out to dry on a line outside of many tin houses and kids waved to us from the side of the roads, jumping up and down. Both girls and boys had shaved heads, so sometimes it was hard to tell them apart from such a young age, unless the girls were wearing dresses, which they often were. The kids ran down red dirt roads, alongside the many goats, cows, and sheep just milling about. Some cows even sat in the gardens, next to their owners, kind of like the family pet. We passed by villages where signs for "Rhino Paint" and "Zebra Hotel" popped up from time to time.

In watching the kids, I felt suddenly overwhelmed with sadness for them as most of them were living in my definition of poverty. However, in saying that, the kids didn't look unhappy at all. Here, they were taking pleasure in the simple things like playing in the dirt and kicking around cans for fun. In fact, they smiled and waved a lot and were the friendliest kids I had ever seen. A smile went a long way; it was an instant connection, a bridge across all barriers. A couple of kids even yelled out "take my picture!" and "how are you?"

Fires flickered in a few yards; perhaps they were burning trash. The smoke curled up towards the endless blue sky. Women with matching head scarves and dresses in bright patterns sold potatoes and carrots along the side of the road. I even saw one of them chase a car that was slowing down to see if they would purchase some veggies from them. Stocky grandmothers sold fruit from ramshackle huts along the side of the dusty road as well, a variety of passion fruit, bananas, and mangos. The air smelled of diesel fuel and dust hung thick in the air. I blew my nose and nothing but dirt came out.

We arrived at the campsite late in the day. A roll of thunder grumbled in the distance. It was going to rain, a bad sign. That was something that didn't go well with camping and was something that I would never get used to…waking up in a musty damp tent.

Chapter Five

"To Uganda, the Pearl of Africa"

We were off to the equator and Uganda beckoned. I hoped for warmer weather since we would be closer to the equator. Kenya was very chilly at night and I wasn't prepared for it. I wasn't sure if it was because it was still spring or if it was because of the elevation.

From our campsite at Eldorat, it took about four hours to reach the Kenyan/Ugandan border. When we arrived, vendors of all ages, from children to adults, crowded around the truck, selling bottles of coke and fried samosas. Children worked here, it was a simple fact. Not all of them of course, but some. The truck was parked and we got off to go through immigration. There seemed to be no system of lining up at the immigration check point and locals pushed in front of us, ignoring any unspoken rules about lining up properly. Perhaps they thought we wouldn't have the guts to say anything if they snuck in front of us in line. And they were right. The most I could do to ward off any oncoming overtakers was to stick my elbows out and stop them in their tracks. But I wasn't about to have an argument in the middle of the crowd. It took ages and when I reached the immigration officer, he threw my departure form in a pile and took off the cover of my passport and tossed it at me over the counter. I was pretty sure he wasn't interested in customer service standards.

On the Ugandan side, it was a bit easier; we all paid 50 USD for a visa and it seemed smooth going compared to the immigration in Kenya. I changed money at the border and had a chat with a banana vendor who looked about five but told me he was twelve years-old. His name was Michael and he was the cutest banana vendor that has probably ever lived. He told me that business was slow but he had a business partner who sold drinks and they split the profits. He was very matter of fact and well-spoken for a twelve year-old. But then again, he also ran his own business. Children going to work was a part of life here and they were seen everywhere, selling drinks and food. Whether it was right or wrong wasn't going to change anything. Financial situations of families determined whether children would work or not. It was as simple as that. By forcing the kids to stop working and going to school instead, would that family suffer from the loss of the income? And by missing school, were these kids fated to end up uneducated and with less opportunities? Of course. These were hard questions demanding good answers. Again, where was the social welfare system?

Once we started driving through Uganda and had gone through the country for a good two hours, I started noticing that the landscape was wilder and lusher than Kenya, overgrown with flowering banana plants that were heavy with large bunches of green bananas. Apparently there were around sixty varieties of bananas in Uganda. It was no wonder that agriculture was Uganda's biggest employer here, with 75% of the population working as farmers. No one should have been going hungry with the kind of perfect soil conditions that Uganda had. The air was warmer as well, I noticed, as the chill that had haunted me since Kenya slowly started to dissipate. The flat landscape was dotted with thatched roof mud huts, some of them huddled together after long stretches of nothing. It was certainly a change from the rusted tin roof huts in Kenya made of scrap metal. It was interesting to see the Ugandans going back to basics with their circular-shaped mud huts made of out of what looked like red clay, and cone tops made of straw. These natural houses seemed to be in better shape than the tin houses I had seen in Kenya.

Another thing I noticed was that the roads were smoother in Uganda than in Kenya. In Kenya, the highways just hadn't been maintained well and were full of potholes. In Uganda, the highways seemed to be well-maintained, but then they would just taper off and turn into red dirt roads, which was kind of strange. It was like the road work had just been abandoned.

Uganda was a small country (similar size as Great Britain) but it has a little bit of everything. They have the tallest mountain range in Africa, the Rwenzories. They also have the Nile River, the world's longest river whose source is said to start in Uganda from Lake Victoria (also shared with Kenya and Tanzania), which also happens to be the African continent's largest lake. Volcanoes that had erupted long ago had caused giant titanic cracks in the earth and those had filled with water, hence there was Lake Victoria, Lake Tanzania, and Lake Malawi. Uganda is also home to about half of all remaining mountain gorillas.

Among Uganda's people, there are two distinct groups, still separated from two waves of migration that made up Uganda's population hundreds of years ago. One of the groups is the Bantu-speaking people who migrated from Western African and who now live in the center of Uganda. The other group was the Nilotic people who migrated to Uganda from Sudan and Ethiopia who are concentrated in the north of Uganda today. And I cannot forget to mention the Batwa pygmies who live in the forests of the southwest.

Uganda has not had an easy or peaceful history, with the most recent reign of terror from Idi Amin in the 70s, who was known as the "butcher of Uganda". One only has to watch "The Last King of Scotland" to get a glimpse of what this crazy man was capable of.

We were heading to Kampala, the country's capital, and would be there by early evening. Kampala had a population of 1.5 million people and, according to travel guides, was not as dangerous as Nairobi. Like Rome, Kampala was known as a city of seven hills, the center of which rests on Nakasero Hill.

We made our way into Kampala sometime in the late afternoon, crossing the wide expanse of the murky and languid Nile River to get there. So far, in both Kenya and Uganda, we had been strictly warned not to take any pictures of any bridges, otherwise, our cameras could be confiscated from us if we were caught. This was military security protocol and although I was tempted to just go ahead and snap a picture of the Nile, I decided that risking losing my camera just wasn't worth it. Entering the outskirts of the city, we passed bleak shanty towns and the dusty backstreets of poverty-stricken townships along the way. This was where the gap between those who had and those who didn't have could be seen clearly. At the townships, it seemed as though everyone in the entire community had gathered together to chat in doorways or while sitting on top of their motorbikes. Townships in Africa are often known for their levels of crime simply due to poverty but again, there was that sense of community that was hard to find outside of it.

Kampala seemed like an oasis rising up in the middle of nowhere, after a day of driving through a sparsely populated landscape. Families zoomed down highways on motorbikes with small toddlers balanced precariously on the laps of the drivers. The crowds of people, the chaos of honking horns, and whining motorbikes were a shock to the senses. The air was full of dust and it smelled of burning wood. Women with African dresses balanced buckets of food on their heads and groups of teens gathered around on street corners, wearing baggy jeans and European football sports shirts. Kids played in the dirt in front of shops and shop fronts were painted with various advertisements for Uganda Telecom, "It's all about U", Sadolin Paint, "Colour Your World", and "Lemon Perfumed Bleach". Buildings were made of concrete and were cracked and run down. Cows tethered with rope munched on overgrown grass. Some of them had really long horns. Palm trees dotted the landscape.

Everything seemed to be covered with a film of red dirt, including myself. We battled the rush hour chaos of traffic and arrived at Red Chili campsite in Kampala after about an hour of driving through the city. I set up my tent while little white monkeys with black faces jumped from branch to branch in the trees above me. They were Vervet monkeys and picked at long string beans growing on the trees. I would have loved to have had one as a domesticated pet but I am sure it was much happier swinging in the trees with its friend. I often think people shouldn't actually buy or have pets unless they can give them a better life than the one they've got already. And these monkeys were perfectly happy and fine where they were.

The campsite had Wi-Fi in its onsite restaurant. While checking my email, a local Ugandan guy who introduced himself as Michael and who was having a Nile Special beer at the next table started to talk to me. He said he was a local but had emigrated to Liverpool, England.

"I'm trying to get a job in Kampala as a project works consultant. I've spoken to several potential employers who all want me to do the job for free. There is no way I am working for no money," he said. "So I'm still looking for potential opportunities for employment. Hopefully, I can get work in Kampala and move back to Uganda permanently."

We spoke at length about micro finance loans. They had been very successful in Africa, especially in villages. However, Michael had a different perspective which made total sense.

"Micro finance loans are given to poor people, who use the loans to satisfy immediate needs, such as hunger, lack of adequate housing, medicine for sick children, etc., not for starting a business," he explained. "The money isn't being used to start small businesses like food stalls, etc. because the money is going to the wrong people who can't pay the loans back."

It was a smaller scale of what happened in the economic downturn of 2008, when too many people decided to default on loan repayments. Michael proposed that the micro finance loans should only be given to people who already had their basic needs met but really and truly needed money to start a business, essentially, the middle class.

"But what about the poor? Who would take care of them?" I proposed.

Michael had no immediate solutions, only that they needed more education so that they could make a life for themselves. He was referring to agricultural education, so these poor people could learn how to grow their own crops, etc. He said Western aid also helped a lot and it was being directed toward solving the immediate needs of the

poverty stricken. But the solution, according to

Michael, was education about agriculture. It made

sense to me but there was no easy solution to how to

relieve poor African countries of their afflictions of

poverty, HIV, and lack of appropriate medical

services. That was for sure.

Chapter Six

"Off to Market We Go!"

The next morning was a free day to do as we pleased. A group of us decided to make our way into the city to see what kind of markets Kampala offered. I was also itching to try some traditional African food. So after brushing my teeth outside my tent to an audience of monkeys, I set off with the rest of the group.

The day was gorgeous and hot with a clear blue sky. The particular market we wanted to go to was advised against by our taxi driver, who said it was too dangerous and there were too many pickpockets. He recommended another one that was a bit smaller. After being dropped off, we got out a map to navigate the streets. Making our way across chaotic roads and squeezing between moving cars, I felt like a target that was at risk of being hit by a moving vehicle at any moment. It was scary and stressful just to cross the street in all that madness. Horns honked and throngs of people were out and about. Rundown cars and *mutatus* full of passengers all competed for space on the roads, as well as pedestrians of all sorts.

We arrived at the overcrowded market, where I was greeted by a foul smell of rotting piles of old vegetables. It hit my nostrils like a punch in the face and was truly an assault to the senses. People were selling a variety of things but mostly fruits and vegetables and what looked like meat that had been sitting out for too long. It wasn't really a market where one would go shopping for a nice African painting. A lot of men walking by immediately asked all the girls in the group, one by one, if we were married or had boyfriends. It was pretty much the worst pick up line I had ever heard. I wondered what they expected, for us to say, "Why no, actually, I'm not married. Would you like to get married?" I mean what were they thinking?!

The market was set up like a maze, with a web of stalls and small alleyways that seemed to lead to nowhere. Again, the smells that came from the stalls I can't say were very pleasant. It was a combination of putrid, decomposed meat and a sour vegetable smell. The food being sold at the market ranged from fried grasshoppers to pigs livers, which looked like a varied diet, if I may say so myself. Apparently, the fried grasshoppers were supposed to be delicious. Locals at the market took great interest in us, or rather I should say what we could *buy* from them. Once they could see that we weren't going to buy anything, they pretty much went back to the business of chatting with the person from the neighboring stall. Africans in general seemed to stare at Westerners but were fairly blasé about it.

"*Jambo*!" a woman in a beautiful African dress greeted me warmly as I walked by.

"*Jambo*! I like your dress," I replied.

"*Asante*," she said, thanking me.

Because of leering men, the market in general felt slightly unsafe and I had to keep an eye on my belongings as we advanced further and further into it. After walking around for a while, we left the market and its smells and made our way up the street, back towards the main road where there were more businesspeople and restaurants. It wasn't long until we found a lovely restaurant overlooking the busy street below.

"*Karibou*," the staff called out as we entered. *Welcome*.

It was full of locals and it served African food, two requirements which I considered to be essential for what I was looking for. Ugandan food was somewhat similar to Kenyan food, except in Uganda *ugali* (a food staple usually made from maize flour) is called *posho*, and is far less popular than *matooke* (mashed plantains). However, one uniquely Ugandan food is the *rolex*, a chapatti rolled around an omelet. There was also the local beer which was popular, the lighter Bell and stronger Nile Special.

It wasn't long before the food arrived and I thoroughly enjoyed my *motooke* (mashed plantains), *posho* (maize meal dumpling or mash), spinach, sweet potato, rice, and bean curry.

After lunch we made our way through the jumble of streets and stalls selling everything from mobile phones to children's underwear to great piles of second-hand clothes. The second hand clothes were actually Salvation Army/other charity donations from the West. More college university shirts and NBA logo sweatshirts were piled up to sell. It was literally a stall full of charity merchandise. The Salvation Army had simply been relocated.

We eventually found the "Experience Africa" market. It was a Fair-Trade market, meaning that whoever had made the goods had been paid or would be paid a fair deal. This one was full of handicrafts and was much more calm and tourist-orientated. Mostly, all the shops were run by headscarf-clad women who didn't hassle us, which I was quite happy about. I was only hassled by one woman, whose superb sales skills convinced me I *definitely* needed a large wooden beautifully carved salad bowl with two giraffes in the middle. Business was *pole-pole*, she explained and she would really like me to buy the bowl.

In addition to the bowl, I bought a small wooden carving of a giraffe, some artwork, and some reed placemats. I was nearly out of money again. I decided it was the perfect time to get out of the market before it reached the point where I couldn't pay for a taxi ride back to the camp. Then I would really be in trouble.

Chapter Seven

"A Visit to the Orphanage"

I woke up around 7:30 A.M. in Kabale, Uganda. We had left Kampala the previous day and had arrived in misty Kabale the previous evening. Kabale was located in Western Uganda, only six miles from the Rwandan border. It was a beautiful area, with lush, green terraced vegetable fields in contrast to the flatter landscape of Eastern Uganda. The morning grass was covered with cold dew and mist moved slowly along the terraced fields from my viewpoint.

Today I was going to a children's orphanage located next to Lake Buyoni. Buyoni meant "place of little birds" and the lake was rumored to be a beautiful location. We piled into a minibus with our driver, who kept saying what sounded like, "make sure you have your nipples with you". But what he really meant was neighbors. After leaving Kabale, we drove through some heavily forested uplands and passed by a lot of people sitting atop large boulders. Our driver told us that they were making gravel for the roads. The sad thing was that they only had pick axes to do the job and hack away at all of those huge boulders. With those tools, it was going to take a long time to do the job. However, because of those simple tools, people had work and could be more self-reliant.

One charity I had come across in my research about Africa was called "Tools for Self Reliance". Donated and second-hand refurbished tools from the UK were sent to various countries in Africa. The key goal of the charity was to give people the skills and tools to get them out of poverty and into work. Education, skills training, and tools would go a long way towards helping African people who were in poverty get back on their feet. Throwing money at the problem would certainly help but it wouldn't provide any long term solutions. It was only putting a band aid on a gaping wound.

Arriving closer to the lake, we drove up a narrow and winding dirt road with a sheer drop on the other side. At the top, green and graceful terraced fields across the valley looked like a staircase to the deep blue sky. Lake Buyoni looked like a blue puddle at the bottom of this valley, surrounded by these steep emerald mountains. One volcanic mountain stood above them all, its top shrouded in mist. That was where the gorillas lived, the guide explained.

We continued along our way until we reached the peaceful shore of the lake. The locals walking down the dusty road looked on in curiosity. One small girl of about six holding a baby in a raggedy blanket asked me to take her picture but I didn't want to in case she wanted something in exchange. A few long wooden boats that resembled long canoes waited for us and we were ushered into them. The orphanage was on the other side of the lake so we would have to cross the lake by boat.

In the boats, we glided towards the other side of the lake, a giant terraced hill dotted with small mud huts and vegetable gardens. The lake was beautiful; the sun glinted off the surface and the water rippled in the breeze. We soon reached the other side of the lake and began our ascent up the steep and muddy hill. It was clear that it had recently rained. It was a long walk but along the way, we were greeted by various children of all ages. Some of them grabbed our hands and asked us what our names were. They were dressed in tatters but they seemed very happy. We passed two other children along the narrow, muddy trail who must not have been over 3 years old, pulling palm fronds along the path that were piled with rocks. They didn't look so happy. I guessed that farm work started early for these kids. We were walking among the terraced fields along the side of the mountain that we had been viewing from the top of the hill across the valley previously. It was a whole different world on the mountain side with gardens and small mud huts. People lived off the land here and tended to their gardens. It was quiet and peaceful. Closer to the top, there was a beautiful view of the lake.

We reached the orphanage before long, which was located along the side of the mountain but close to the top. There were two simple one-room mud buildings and a few mud huts huddled together. In one building, kids dressed in shaggy but clean school uniforms sat at wooden desks doing multiplication timetables. This was the orphanage school. The kids were adorable and smiled at us with toothy grins.

Their middle-aged female teacher then led them into a few songs in which they performed various actions such as sitting, standing, tapping on each other's shoulders, etc. Some of the songs were about Jesus and praying and others had more of an African beat.

Christianity had played a big presence in sub-Saharan Africa due to the missionaries and it was certainly a place where Christianity was *growing*. According to the Pew Research Center's "Global Christianity" report in 2011, which has been billed as the most comprehensive and reliable study to date, major shifts have occurred since 1910, when two-thirds of the world's Christians lived in Europe. Now only one in four Christians lived in Europe. The rest were distributed across the Americas (37 %), sub-Saharan Africa (24 %) and the Asia-Pacific region (13 %). In Africa, Christianity and Islam existed side by side and although Christianity traced its beginnings to the Middle East and North Africa, only 4% of residents in those regions claimed the Christian faith today.

After listening to the kids sing, we were then led outside and made a large circle. The kids were going to dance for us. And *dance* they did. They were naturals, and could move well to the beats of the songs which were all sung by the other children. There were no iPod docking systems here, or even electricity for that matter; the kids made their own music. There were two girls in particular that led the song and dance, shaking their hips energetically. I was sure they were no more than seven years old. No sooner did I wish that I could dance like these girls, than one of them actually pulled me into the center of the circle. I did my best to keep up with her and was having so much fun that I nearly forgot that I was still in the center of the circle. I had to step back and let someone else have a turn. After a while, I was beginning to understand the moves and words and after that, there was no stopping me. I danced with little kids of all ages and they were so fun to dance with because they were so involved, everything they did was with so much energy and effort. I had forgotten how much energy that kids had.

Somewhere in the process of the whole thing, I acquired a little shadow, a little boy with big eyes who grasped onto my hand and followed me everywhere. He simply stared up at me with those big round eyes looking quite sad. I could tell he was shy. He shadowed my dance moves. Even when I shrugged my shoulders and stuck out my tongue, he mimicked them. The two girls leading the group were such good singers and dancers that they scared away the boys when they approached them. It was a great time and I was sad when the dancing ended due to a monsoonal torrential rain pour that sent everyone scurrying for shelter. The storm rattled the mountain with a blast of rain, thunder, and flashes of white lightening. I wondered how we would get back down the hill, walking or sliding?

We huddled inside one of the one-room buildings with the kids as their attention drifted to various peoples' possessions such as cameras, iPhones, sunglasses, and watches. They wanted to look at our pictures, take pictures with our cameras, and wear our sunglasses and watches. They were genuinely interested in these items that they probably didn't get much access to. Among the kids was an 18 year-old rapper named Lubadubba.

"I am Lubadubba and I love to rap," he said, after giving me a quick demonstration of his skills. "I need sponsors though. I need a microphone, guitar, Adidas tracksuit pants, and Converse high top shoes so I can be a proper rapper. And twenty people to be in my music video. I need dancers. Yah."

I had noticed that the Africans often said "yah" a lot which meant yes, yeah, ok. I liked it.

There was a pile of bricks in the corner of the one-room building so I sat on the top to see if I could get a better vantage point of the kids as they were swarming around me. Even on the top of the bricks, they had soon surrounded me. We were soon called for lunch. We were eating at the orphanage manager's home and followed him down a path that resembled a shallow river now. His home was a simple mud brick hut with only enough seats for about ten people. He served us crayfish curry (which tasted like jambalaya), mixed vegetables, rice, potatoes, and stewed chicken in a tomato sauce. It was an absolute feast.

"How long does it take to build these kinds of houses?" I asked about his one-room brick house.

"Only two months," he replied. "The usual one-room, simple mud huts only takes three weeks. The mud is mixed with concrete and then made into bricks. This is how the whole house doesn't come down in a torrential downpour."

The manager told us that they were trying to raise money to build another school and needed about $2,500. It wasn't much and was certainly attainable with donations.

Our tour leaders told us that they were wary of other orphanage managers who they had met previously, mostly because these managers were living in nice homes with flat screen TVs and wearing nice watches and shoes. Edison, the owner of the orphanage we had visited, of course, had none of this and lived simply. He was quite passionate about taking care of the kids.

Lunch was delicious, and after we were all finished, we made our way very carefully down the steep slope, sometimes sliding. Some of the kids followed us and I hoped no one would grab my hand this time, simply because at the moment, I was a liability going down the hill and I would take anyone down with me. I think they knew that and not one of them attempted to hold my hand this time. We soon reached the bottom and piled back into the boats. I trailed my hand in the water, it was cool and inviting. We reached the other side of the lake after a few minutes.

Back at the campsite later, some people who had accidentally left their tents open in the torrential downpour, now found that the inside of their tents had been flooded and their stuff was soaking wet. My rain cover flap was down so I was safe despite a small puddle at the opening of the tent. Even though my stuff wasn't soaked, the tent smelled musty and wet. It wasn't the nicest smell. I spent the next hour cleaning out the puddles in the tent and setting my stuff up. It was hard enough to camp when it was cold, but wet and cold would drive one crazy. Once you got something wet while camping, it was hard to get the musty smell out of it.

I went to the shower to wash off my legs and feet from the mud from the mountain. As I turned the knob for hot water, the entire thing came off into my hands and a stream of hot water flew out of the pipe at me. I frantically tried to get the knob back on the shower but I was unable to turn the water off. It was now coming out in a stream from the wall where the pipe came out of.

I was fully clothed so ran outside to grab one of the staff. A guy came into the shower with me and I explained that I was sorry, but the knob had come off and now I couldn't turn off the water.

"Yah," he replied, nodding in understand.

He didn't seem too bothered about the problem.

"What did you do today?" he asked instead, while he was fiddling with the shower knob. "And where are you from?"

"I visited an orphanage today which was nice. Very nice. I am from America"

"Oh, America? I want to go there. Yah."

He managed to turn the large leak into a small one, of which I was grateful for. I just felt bad for the next person to use the shower. Although that's probably what the last person to use the shower had also thought.

Chapter Eight

"Rwanda, Rwanda"

Rwanda was the destination of the day. After we crossed the border (I didn't have to pay a visa fee for Rwanda!), the scenery began to drastically change from low hills to green mountains and lush terraced tea plantations stretching for miles. People walked along the side of the road, with women carrying burlap bags of freshly dug up carrots on their heads and men carrying piles of scrap wood. The foot traffic wasn't as heavy as we had seen in Kenya and Uganda but the interesting thing about these people was that they were even friendlier than those we had seen in the previous two countries. It was the first thing that struck me about Rwanda, that despite its horribly sad past filled with civil war between two tribes, people were smiling and waving. Previously, it had just been kids waving to us with occasional adults as well. But in Rwanda, it seemed that *everyone* waved, even adults working in the tea plantations. People stopped working to wave!

There were endless rows of tea, perfect in straight lines. Tall gum trees with peeling bark lined the sides of the road and misty emerald mountains dotted with patches of coffee-colored brown and red dirt surrounded us on all sides. The terraced mountains held a variety of crops and the road we followed twisted through them. Hand-built houses made from mud bricks with Spanish-style villa roofs dotted the lush hills. The houses seemed to be better constructed than the mud huts of Uganda and also better than the rusted tin houses in Kenya. Wild and thin palm trees grew in clusters where there were no crops and they swayed in the cool breeze. The air smelled fresh, and as we drove further, the peaks got

higher and the mountains seemed to go on forever.
Gardens and crops were planted on terraced fields all
the way to the top of the mountain. These people were
making use of the land, that was for sure. Every inch
of it was covered by some sort of crop. I imagined the
people at the top were pretty self-sufficient, otherwise
that was a hell of a long way to the grocery store. We
passed tiny villages with small shops whose signs
plastered to its walls said "meals taste better with
Coke" and "Primus beer".

I had noticed already that there were fewer
animals in Rwanda than there had been in previous
countries. No one was selling fruit and vegetables
along the road either (maybe they kept it for
themselves?). But one thing was certain, the people
were definitely friendlier. Sometimes the kids would
even spot us and run after the truck with glee. Some
people held their hands out along the side of the road

as if to say, "give me some money", which is surely what they intended. Most people in the countryside seemed to be working in the fields and I didn't see people laying around and not doing anything like I had seen in Kenya and Uganda. The signs were in French, as Rwanda used to be a colony of Belgium.

A pygmy man carrying a battery shouted for money along the side of the road, laughing. The pygmies had really had it hard in Rwanda. They were a tribe of people who were quite small and were treated like outcasts by the rest of the regular-sized Rwandans. The pygmies were once hunter-gatherers in the forests of Rwanda but their way of living differed from that of the general population. For that they have been marginalized and this has resulted in near extinction of these people. In 1998, the Pygmies lost their home in the Nyungwe Forest and the Volcanoes National Park because it was created to be a sanctuary for the mountain gorillas. Both groups are in danger of becoming extinct, one, a group of animals, the other, humans.

After the Rwandan genocide of 1994, all ethnic identification was outlawed by the Rwandan government, to decrease the chances that another ethnic war would break out. The people were no longer of this or that tribe, but were now all Rwandans. Now, the pygmies official name was the "Community of Potters" in order to be recognized by the government.

We arrived around noon in Kigali, the capital city of Rwanda. It seemed crazy and chaotic like other African capital cities, but there was something about it that suggested it was a little better off than Kampala, Uganda or Nairobi in Kenya. Perhaps after the genocide, Rwanda had to rebuild itself as a nation and that's why some of the buildings were looking newer. Having watched "Hotel Rwanda" several years prior, I really wanted to see the Hotel des Mille Collines, the inspiration for the film, where tragic events of the genocide once played out.

We were soon at the genocide memorial, dedicated to the Hutus and Tutsis who had been involved in a civil war, with Tutsis killing children with machetes, raping women and giving them AIDS, and killing every Hutu in site. Close to one million people were murdered in three months by the Interahamwe, a terrorist military group. The genocide memorial was well done and it broke my heart to walk through it and read about all the horrible things that had happened to the Rwandans. I couldn't imagine living on after such a tragedy and having to learn to let the past go, as well as trying to live with the people who had murdered family and friends. I wanted to commend the Rwandans for trying to move on as a unified nation, instead of focusing on who was from what tribe and from where. It would be a hard thing to let go, especially if tribal affiliations had gone on for so long.

Genocide memorials were certainly not an enjoyable experience but were something that had to be done, no matter if you were visiting the concentration camps in Germany or the Khmer Rouge killing fields in Cambodia. Everyone needed to know and never forget about the atrocities that human beings were capable of committing. History was an important thing to study, so we could prevent mistakes like these from happening again. I briefly remembered the Billy Joel song, "We Didn't Start the Fire", about how humans have always been fighting since the beginning of time. Civil wars, tribal wars, wars between neighboring countries, and world wars have been headlines for as long as anyone from any century could remember if asked. The world has been fighting since the beginning. History shows this and although we may not be able to prevent people from fighting, studying history at least helps us to *try*.

After the memorial, we drove on. It was going to be a really long day. Some people in the group were going gorilla trekking the following day, in the Virunga Mountains. We moved on, passing more and more terraced fields and green lush mountains that grew in size. Women carried baskets on their heads and with the surrounding environment; it was surreal to think about being here.

We soon spotted the volcanic mountains where the gorillas lived. We were getting closer to camp. The town of Musanze, at the foot of these mountains, greeted us. It looked like it was better off than other small towns in Africa, perhaps because of all the tourist dollars flooding in. One permit to trek to see the gorillas was $500 and some of that money went back into the community. I unfortunately hadn't budgeted for seeing the mountain gorillas as I was spending three months in Africa already.

We arrived at camp a few minutes later. It was a former monastery for Catholic monks and had a bar and facilities for laundry, etc. I headed to the bar to try Primus, Rwanda's national beer. The Primus was nice, both refreshing and light. I liked it better than the Nile Special. I gazed over the bar menu. The food seemed similar to that in Uganda with goat, chicken, and beef paired with ugali (maize meal) and matoke (mashed plantains). It was time to try some local food.

***

The next day the few of us that were left behind went to go explore the town while the others went to see the mountain gorillas. I really wished that I had signed up to do that but it just wasn't possible since I had decided the trade-off was to see more of Africa itself.

Musanze was in the most mountainous region of Rwanda and was the biggest part of Volcanos National Park. It was settled at the foot of a range of misty volcanic mountains which lent to its charm. The town's infrastructure was better maintained due to all the tourist dollars flooding in from the mountain gorillas. Motorcycle drivers yelled out, "sister, sister!" to me as I walked by them, hoping I would take them up on a ride into town. To the guys they yelled out, "hey brother from a different mother!" It was all very friendly but I could tell that they were not going to get much business because the sky was full of rain-heavy clouds that seemed ready to unleash on us at any minute. We found our way to a little French bakery that had very strong Rwandan coffee. I ordered a coffee and an omelet and fries. The service was extremely slow. I think the food took over an hour to come out and everyone moved at the pace of a snail. And we were the only customers. *Pole-pole.*

***

The next morning we left Rwanda to head back to Uganda. The clouds had cleared in Rwanda, but as soon as we crossed the border into Uganda, around noon, I swear the clouds were back. I was starting to feel like there were ten seasons in one day. You could never tell what to expect.

At one point we were really close to the border of the Democratic Republic of Congo and passed a refugee camp that looked so bleak in the rain. It was full of refugees from the DRC. It was something that you might see on the nightly news but never in real life and I was seeing it in real time. Refugees had come into neighboring countries and had been displaced from their homes in the DRC. This was because of three groups of terrorist military organizations roaming around the country and generally raping and killing wherever they went. It was a horrible situation. Safety is a basic need and the people living at the refugee camps had experienced so much fear already. How would things ever return to "normal" for them?

Chapter Nine

"Adventures in Jinja, Uganda"

We were heading to Jinja, the adventure capital of Uganda. Jinja is the largest city in the east of Uganda and has some of the world's best white-water rafting on its doorstep. Jinja is also rumored to be the source of the Nile River.

I looked out the window, lost in my own world and Africa. Cows with long horns grazed in fields of vegetables and in front of mud huts, flicking their tails. Trucks honked their horns as they passed us, groups of young men sat on steps and chatted; the day had already started for many Ugandans. We passed through Kampala again and I saw signs advertising that a person could buy a 3-5 bedroom house in Kampala for 160,000 USD! In some parts of

America, you could buy a house for cheaper and I was sure that you would get more for your money.

Boda bodas (motorbikes) zoomed by us on the road and the traffic in Kampala was chaotic. We were soon stopping at a large supermarket to pick up supplies, which I was absolutely thrilled about. While I was shopping for the goods, I heard one of the shop staff singing Adele's "Someone Like You" in the supermarket aisle. I really wanted to start singing with him but in the end I didn't because there were people around. I think we could have made a nice duet. I really wish I had done it.

We arrived at Jinja camp, which was really nice and overlooked the Nile River (the Nile River!) and had a bar, restaurant, shower facilities, and a small library where you could exchange books. For dinner, I joined the others at the restaurant and noticed that it was really unfortunate that none of the restaurants at the campsites had local African dishes. I would have loved to tuck into some ugali and bean curry.

***

The next morning I walked down the road from the campsite to get a *chapati*. *Chapatis* were basically what I thought of as breakfast burritos; Indian flatbread (similar to a tortilla) with veggies and egg, cooked and rolled up, "burrito" style. Unfortunately, it was pouring. One benefit of the camp was that it sat on the top of a hill overlooking the Nile River. It was a beautiful view, that's for sure. The brown Nile moved languidly, with green hills rising up on both sides. Some small paddle boats were on the river and crocs were rumored to be in the water, but no one had seen them in these parts.

It rained and rained but cleared up sometime in the afternoon. A few of us took a walk down to the Nile and I dipped my toes in it. A couple of local barefoot African boys dressed in shabby but clean clothes in a paddle boat on the Nile noticed us and rowed over.

"*Jambo!*" they shouted to us.

"*Jambo!*" we shouted back and then decided to walk back up to the camp.

The boys followed me. "You give us tour?" they asked, which I thought was strange. It was clear that they were scouting the place out for some unknown reason.

"You take picture of me?" one of them asked. "Please show me."

I took a picture of them and then showed them on the camera. For some reason, the kids in Africa loved having their pictures taken and then loved to see it afterwards. They found it fascinating.

The boys said they lived across the river, in a poor village. They told me that their family owned a *duka* (shop) that sold a few things like vegetables, flour, rice, maize flour, and sugar but that the family didn't have any money.

I asked the boys about their lives in the village and they explained to me that they helped sell vegetables at the *duka*. The boys had been sent to go out and do some fishing but I didn't see them with any poles. They were clearly educated as they spoke good English which was probably more than a lot of the kids in the villages could ask for as many didn't have money for school fees. I was amazed with the people in Africa and their language abilities in English. I'm not sure what I was expecting but it certainly wasn't that so many locals could speak really good English.

I wondered why the boys weren't in school on that particular day.

"We have to stay home today to help out with the family business. Mother is working in the garden."

It was a fact in Uganda that 87% of the farm labor consists of women but only 5% of the land is owned by them.

"Can you buy?" they asked me, producing a fire extinguisher out of a plastic sack.

"I'm sorry but I don't have any room in my bag for that," I explained.

Where they got it was hard to say. They eventually walked away, showing way too much interest in people's clothes drying on the clothesline. The security guards noticed them and told them to leave. On the way out, they seriously asked one of the girls if she would like to trade any clothing with them. Perhaps they wanted to give a gift to their mothers or sisters. It was hard to not feel sorry for them.

Later that night, after a dinner of a delicious White Nile Perch with Kenyan coconut sauce on the top, I chatted with one of the local African staff working at the bar who was a dead ringer for the lead singer of Bloc Party, Kele Okereke. He told me he loved his job and had a lot of fun.

"I feel very lucky to have this job. I am on a high salary for a typical Ugandan. I make one dollar an hour. With this, I can help my family."

He still lived with his parents and brothers and sisters in Jinja. Here was a success story of a middle-class Ugandan who was happy with life. He also only ever had malaria once in his entire life. Now *that* was lucky.

Chapter Ten

"Hungry Hippos"

We were on our way back to Kenya for more sightseeing, completing a loop before heading to Tanzania. Once we had crossed the border, I gazed out the window at the Kenyan scenery. There were plateaus and vast expanses of scrub and semi-arid landscape dotted with the signature African tree, the acacia. I decided I liked Kenyan scenery the best so far, it seemed the most "African" to me. It resembled the Africa of storybooks and paintings. Although both Uganda and Rwanda had beautiful, lush scenery and not a blade of dead grass in comparison to Kenya's sparse environment, I liked what I saw in Kenya.

The last few weeks we had been on the move almost every day. This meant taking down and putting up tents constantly, taking cold showers, and getting wet and cold at all hours in the constant rain (I couldn't remember the last time I had warm feet). My hands and feet were like lumps of ice and had been since we had left the equator. Everyone was getting ill with stomach bugs, colds, and general sicknesses. The trip certainly couldn't be considered what most people thought of as a vacation, which is synonymous with relaxing. It all depended on what you would consider a vacation. Traveling was tiring. But it *was* an adventure.

We arrived at Fisherman's Camp, which was set on the shores of Lake Naivasha, late in the afternoon on a cold and dreary day. The camp was huge and seemed like a national park in itself, with monkeys jumping from branch to branch in the trees overhead and rumors of hippos coming out to feed at dusk. I set up my tent and went to explore. The monkeys jumping in the trees had very long tails and a white fringe of fur on their black bodies. They were called colubus monkeys. Extremely large storks stood on their stick legs in the shallow park of the brownish green lake.

The air was cool and crisp, the grass constantly covered in dew, even late in the day. The smell of campfire smoke wafted through the air from around the campsite. I joined some others in our group for a beer as they made a fire. The fire felt so nice after being so cold and wet and I finally felt dry for the first time in days. I sat by the fire until dinner. The following day we were going to Crater Lake, where we would be going on a walking safari, with sightings of a variety of animals like zebras, wildebeest, and giraffes, and also taking a boat out to see hippos. I couldn't wait.

***

The next morning, I managed to get ready in 20 minutes and met everyone else along with the guide, George. We piled into a very tiny minivan whose bumper read "you can't touch this" (MC Hammer tribute perhaps?). George was tall, slim, and well-dressed. He didn't smile or talk much however (two requirements for a guide, right?).

On the other hand, he did know everything about the animals if asked but no knowledge was shared voluntarily. As we drove to the Crater Lake, I actually spotted some zebras and giraffe along the side of the road. I really couldn't believe it; they were just there in the open spaces. There were no fences in Africa, all these wild animals roamed freely. The scenery was beautiful along the way, with savannah stretching to low lying hills in the distance. It wasn't long before we arrived to the Crater Lake National Park, where we would begin our walking safari. Crater Lake was called as such because there was a lake on the bottom of an extinct volcano on the western side of Lake Naivasha inside the park. The lake was the color of jade and was said to be held in high regard by the local Maasai people, who believed that its water helped soothe ailing cattle.

The next four or so hours were magical, a once in a lifetime experience. We walked among zebras, giraffes with their babies, warthogs (who were skittish and wouldn't let us get close), one wildebeest, baboons, and antelope (ranging from eland to gazelle to dik-dik which were the smallest antelope and about the size of a Chihuahua). It was great to be on the ground with them and walking through the wild and dusty scrub of the African bush in its entire untamed splendor. There was a different feel when you were on the ground with these beautiful creatures and they also could make you feel so small, especially the giraffes. There was also the strange feeling of being in the solace of untrammeled wilderness of this kind and hearing nothing but the swish, crunch, and snap of the twigs and scrub underneath your feet. The zebras and giraffes weren't too bothered about our presence, as long as we kept a fair distance from them. I ventured as close as I could to a zebra but it just nodded its head at me as if to say, "Yes, that's too close so back off please."

I really enjoyed watching the giraffes. The adults actually kissed their young on the top of their heads. I watched them in amusement. Giraffes and zebras seemed to stick together. George said it was because they thought each other's patterns were attractive. They were both very fashionable animals so I couldn't think of a better reason to be friends.

Well, that and the fact that both species were vegetarians. That was what really mattered in this world of the animal kingdom. You had to be careful who you made friends with.

The weather was absolutely perfect, it couldn't have been better. It was the first dry and sunny day we had had in a long time and although it was hot as horseradish, it felt wonderful with the sun beating down on us from the wide African sky. We trekked for about four hours, animal spotting, and then headed to the top of a volcano for a lookout over the landscape and the jade-colored Crater Lake. It was gorgeous, stretching far and wide to the green hills in the distance. George said there was one hippo that was stuck inside the Crater Lake that had somehow gotten in there when the plains had flooded. I guessed that was one lonely hippo.

After the lookout, we got into the van and headed down a dusty road to Lake Naivasha. When we arrived there, I literally had to shake the dust off of myself; I was covered from head to toe in it. We walked to the shore of Lake Naivasha in order to be taken out to see the hippos. Herds of cattle drank from the edge of the lake and goats ran about, minded by a herder, who walked around with a long stick. Cows drank and kids swam near them while women washed clothes. It was a meeting of animals and people at one spot.

We hopped in a small motor boat and set away from the shore. The lake was a greenish color and surrounded by green low hills. A line of pink stretched out on the horizon. It was a perfect line of pink flamingos floating in perfect symmetry. The sky seemed huge ahead and was a bright baby blue color. Antelopes and zebra could be seen grazing on the nearby hills and the moment was purely African fantasy.

Something bobbed in the water and that's when I realized that we were next to a group of about twenty hippos. They gazed at us with a bit of interest but otherwise didn't seem too bothered considering their extreme dislike of humans. They bobbed and dipped underwater before coming up with the sound of something letting out a huge gust of air. They had tiny ears and sometimes you could see a glimpse of their body as they floated in the water or changed positions. It was hard to imagine them as being incredibly dangerous as they sat staring at us with unblinking eyes and small heads (in comparison to their bodies).

We moved on, spotting more hippos further down the lake. A flock of flamingos went airborne as we approached, resembling long pink sticks with wings. I thought they were beautiful in flight, with their wing colors of pink and black flashing against the backdrop of the blue sky. Flamingoes seemed a little skittish to me, they all took off into the air and settled into a new spot on the water not too far away. And when one went, they all went. I felt sorry that they had to keep moving. But, this was just another day in Africa.

Chapter Eleven

"Nairobi Shock"

We arrived back in dirty and dusty Nairobi in the late afternoon the following day after our Crater Lake walk by Lake Naivasha. Nairobi was a shock to the senses after the wilderness of rural Kenya. Sounds of honking horns and the whine of motorbikes overtook my senses. We arrived at Karen camp, exactly where we had started our trip three weeks before. It felt strange going back there after what we had seen and done.

Some people had decided to visit a local elephant sanctuary but I decided to skip it since I would be seeing elephants in the wild. I wanted to get out and about and see Nairobi while I had the chance. Unfortunately, many of the elephants at the sanctuary had been orphaned because the parents had been killed by poachers. I couldn't believe that was still going on. Apparently, elephant tusks were getting even more popular because in Asia, there was Chinese medicine that was made from the ivory that was said to increase the male erection, like Viagra. I wondered why the Chinese didn't just take Viagra instead of poaching endangered animals for their ivory. It was time to start spreading the rumor that the ivory in the medicine had the opposite effect from what they wanted.

I headed to the Galleria mall to have a look around. The malls in Kenya were surrounded by security and police checking each car for bombs. Since 2012, Kenya had seen an upsurge in violent terrorist attacks. The Kenyan security forces believed that the blasts were carried out by Al-Shabaab in retaliation for Operation Linda Nchi, a coordinated military mission between the Somalian military, the

Kenyan military, the Ethiopian military, the French military, and the United States military that began in October 2011, when troops from Kenya crossed the border into the conflict zones of southern Somalia.

The soldiers were in pursuit of Al-Shabaab militants who were alleged to have kidnapped several foreign tourists and aid workers inside Kenya. At the urging of Al-Shabaab, an increasing number of terrorist attacks in Kenya had been carried out by local Kenyans, many of whom were recent converts to Islam. Referred to as the "Kenyan Mujahideen" by Al-Shabaab's core members, the converts are typically young and overzealous, poverty making them easier targets for the outfit's recruitment activities. Because the Kenyan insurgents have a different profile from the Somali and Arab militants that allows them to blend in with the general population of Kenya, they are also often harder to track.

There had been quite a few terrorist bombs going off in Nairobi and it was actually quite scary to see all the security checks going on when you really thought about it. At least they were checking for bombs and car bombs at Galleria before letting people into the parking lot though, that meant that it was a generally a safe place to be. The mall was a nice breath of normality. But the normality left again when I stood in line at the supermarket forever, only to find that when I got to the checkout register, there was some sort of mechanical problem and I had to move to the other line, which was something close to a million miles long. One funny thing about standing in line in Africa was that if there was an African woman behind you in line, she would get so close to you that she was actually touching you, as in pressed up against you. This was very strange for me, this concept of zero personal space in such a large continent with a low population.

On the way back, I chatted with the taxi driver. Amazingly, the guy didn't like Obama because he said that Obama had his chance and not much happened so Mitt Romney should have a chance. This was really rare for a Kenyan to say because they really loved Obama.

"The Chinese are coming here to build roads and factories, as favors to the government. But there is nothing free in this world, right?" he asked me, looking at me in the rearview mirror. "The Chinese will expect something in return for this big favor. Maybe they will build more factories and have more ownership of land here. This is a worry for Kenyans. Will the government sell all of our land to the Chinese? They will own us. Maybe they will help us build our country up but maybe they will also own us then."

The taxi driver knew quite a bit about Kenyan politics. He believed the Kenyan government was corrupt. He wished that the Kenyans could do what the Chinese were doing. What he meant was that he wished that instead of bringing the Chinese in to build the roads, he wished that the locals could do it.

He also spoke about the tribal wars between the various tribes of Kenya and the difficulty in uniting many groups of people under the label of "Kenyan". I guessed there was no perfect solution. All I knew was that it was an African problem and one that could only be solved by Africans for the solution to work.

Chapter Twelve

"A Bowl of Animals"

Tanzania. Its history began with the dawn of humanity. Hominid (humanlike) footprints found in the Tanzanian plains showed that our earliest ancestors were roaming here over three million years ago. The humans who roam Tanzania today are quite peaceful. Unlike Kenya and other surrounding neighbors, tribal rivalries are almost nonexistent. Tanzania is a multicultural country in terms of its makeup of various African tribes as well as Christians and Muslims, who also live side by side quite peacefully here. Tanzanians, like many other African countries, give great respect to their elders and strangers are greeted and called as sister, brother, mama, or comrade.

The country also has no shortage of amazing sites including Kilimanjaro, Ngorongoro Crater, Serengeti National Park, and the beautiful island of Zanzibar in the turquoise seas of the Indian Ocean. In many of these amazing sites you can see all the best of African wildlife ranging from elephants to lions to rhinos to cheetahs to hyenas to hippos to zebra to antelope to buffalo to giraffes. Dare I go on?

For the reasons listed above, and for many others, I found myself in Tanzania. We crossed the border and made our way to Arusha, to be exact. Arusha was better well-developed than other parts of Tanzania that didn't happen to be on the safari circuit. Here, roads were well-maintained all the way to the Serengeti. Unfortunately, in the far flung regions of Tanzania, where there were no tourist dollars, pounds, or euros flowing in, roads weren't good and infrastructure remained broken.

On the morning of the first full day in Tanzania, a group of six of us spoke with the South African woman who owned the camp. She recommended a guide who would take us all to the Ngorongoro Crater, one of the most amazing wildlife spotting places in Africa.

The Crater was one part of a large area of interrelated ecosystems, of collapsed volcanoes, alkaline lakes, gorges, and volcanoes. The Crater itself was a caldera, a collapsed volcano about 12 miles wide and it held the grazing grounds of a multitude of wild animals including lions, elephants, buffaloes, flamingos, and black rhinos. Local Maasai had grazing rights there as well and it wasn't uncommon to see them tending to their cattle around the area. I just hoped they steered clear of the lions.

We would depart the following day, but first, we needed to go into Arusha and meet the guide and give him the money for the day trip so he could secure our permits to enter the park. Arusha was the gateway city to Tanzania's northern safari circuit and it had seen its fair share of tourists. We were staying about thirty minutes away from Arusha and the ride to get there passed by mostly maize and wheat fields. The town was named after one of the local tribes, the Arusha people, who tended the very land that we passed.

Upon arrival to Arusha, the group of us spent the rest of the day sorting out getting the guide money, etc. for the following day and having a look at the local markets after a lunch of bean curry and stewed cabbage. At the market, I was immediately latched onto by a few vendors who seemed desperate for my business. One of them was a guy who was extremely interested in getting me to buy some sunglasses that I had merely glanced at. The guy wanted 30 dollars for a pair of cheap plastic sunglasses that were nothing special. I finally told him that I would give him 5 dollars and nothing else. I didn't even want them but this guy, named John, knew how to apply sales pressure. He agreed on five dollars and the sunglasses were mine. Next, he wanted me to buy a bracelet. I could tell it was going to go on and on.

The market was bustling, with people haggling for fruits and vegetables. There were flashes of color everywhere, from spices to beans to veggies to clothes. Someone grabbed my hand and I yelled out. A man laughed as I walked by. An old woman with cataract eyes walked through the market shouting "hallelujah" and John told me she was preaching about sin. She carried a bible and sounded extremely angry. Everyone wanted us to buy something from them but I had already bought the sunglasses and that was enough.

I escaped into a shopping area where a security guard shooed out John, who was still following me. All I could do was breathe a sigh of relief.

***

Our guide arrived at 7 A.M. to pick us up and soon we were on our way and out into the endless stretch of African savannah. The Ngorongoro Crater was about 124 miles from Arusha so it was going to be a long drive. The countryside of Tanzania looked like the Africa I had always imagined, even more so than Kenya, with flat top acacia trees and dry, semi-arid scrubby landscape, with grey mountains in the distance. Mud huts of Maasai villages dotted the landscape. Everywhere, walking along the road and also in villages, were Maasai people. It was a real African experience. We passed by Lake Manyara, which was located on the edge of a salt flat. The semi-arid landscape held bottle trees, red dirt, and purple bougainvillea. Maasai men slapped the behinds of the animals they herded along the sides of the roads to keep them moving. Red tuk-tuks zoomed through small villages, the first I had seen in Africa. There was an intense dry heat that seemed to permeate everything and the land shimmered in the distance with the heat. It was a heat that made your eyes water and your nostrils go so dry that they cracked and bled.

At one point, we got stuck behind a vehicle with a decal of J-Lo and P-Diddy that said "hoodlum". We climbed up the crater slowly behind this vehicle until we reached the top and stopped to look out. The Crater was a large abyss in the ground the shape of a bowl, it literally was a crater, a collapsed volcano, surrounded by green mountains with a flat floor dotted with very few trees and salty-looking lakes. It was a showplace of evolution's slow magic, an ancient and raw frontier. I could see dots, which were animals, but they were the size of ants from where I was standing on the top. It was a beautiful and stunning windswept expanse.

From the top, there was only one way to go and that was down into this giant bowl. We made our way to the crater floor which took about an hour, as we were so far up. As we neared the bottom I could see grassland stretching for miles and hardly a tree in sight. A couple of spotted hyenas crossed in front of us, looking sneaky as they crept through the tall grass. A huge ostrich pranced to the left, its black feathers rustling in the wind. Beyond it were zebras that merely looked at us with disinterest and continued munching away at the endless expanse of golden flaxen grass.

Our game drive truck was a Land Rover with a top that opened up so everyone could poke their heads up and see. Further along I spotted what I had wanted to see the whole time, a lion - or in this case a lioness! This particular muscular lioness was eating an African buffalo, which by the looks of things, had been freshly killed. The lioness looked full and almost sick, heaving with each breath. Her teeth and large paws were bloody and it looked like she had bitten off more than she could chew (literally). We watched her for a while and she didn't even take notice of us. A little ways away was a male and female lion couple. From what we had heard from another group passing by us on the road, they had just finished a session of lovemaking. The guide said they did this about twenty times per day and would surely be at it again in a few minutes. We waited and waited and finally saw the male lion attempt it. However, he was rejected by the female and let out an injured howl at the lioness. They both flopped on the grass to lie in the sun. They were beautiful creatures, fierce and docile at the same time. The lion's magnificent full mane of golden brown hair ruffled in the breeze as he lay there with eyes half open. It was amazing to see these stunning creatures, the kings at top of the animal food chain, in their natural habitat.

The bottom of the crater was full of wildebeest; there were hundreds and hundreds of them dotting the floor of this wind-scoured valley. They were the strangest looking animals I had ever seen, a cross between a goat, a donkey and God knows what else. They seemed like they would be easy prey for the lions to attack and eat. And they were. They couldn't outrun them or do much damage to any prey which was quite sad. They were meant to be eaten. It always happened to the vegetarian animals which seemed a little unfair!

A warthog ran among them, with its tiny tail sticking straight into the air. They were certainly adorably ugly creatures. "Pumba" was the name for warthog in Swahili, just like on the Lion King. We saw another warthog soon after, a mother this time, with about four little warthoglets. They were adorable and tiny as youngsters and kept getting uglier as they grew. Their little tails moved back and forth quickly and they never left the mother's side as she foraged for food.

Further down the road a hyena cooled itself in the mud. We pulled up right next to it. It may have even been possible to reach down and touch it but it gave us a cackling hyena laugh as if to say, go away.

Not that anyone would have touched it. It looked like a suspicious mutt with dark eyes. Hyenas have bone-crushing capabilities with their strong jaws and although they are said to be scavengers, a pack of them can easily take down a lion.

The scenery was otherworldly and I felt like I was in the middle of the set for the Lion King. In fact, as I looked at my pictures, I realized that they all looked fake. They were *that* good. The Crater was more or less a bowl of animals. Further on in the distance, a black rhino and two African elephants grazed. We could only spot them on the horizon. Birds fluttered about; hawks, vultures and eagles flew overhead. It was a melting pot of animal cultures.

We drove on to a small lake to have a lunch of butter and cheese sandwiches (sounds kind of weird, but really it's a delicious combination) and bananas. While we were eating, we watched hippos roll around in the water. There were about ten of them. It was like a live version of the Discovery Channel in 3D.

After lunch, we left the lake and moved further on. This time, the elephants had moved closer. They weren't too far away and I could see them clearly, lumbering through the tall grass. An elephant skull sat in the grass a few feet away. I had to pinch myself to believe that I was actually there seeing these animals in the wild. I reaffirmed to myself as we departed the Crater later in the day that it had been one of my top travel experiences of my entire life.

Once we were out of the Crater, we stopped at village about an hour outside to buy Maasai blankets, called *shuka*. They were plaid print and came in colors like orange and green, blue and red, and red and black. The men running the shop were very friendly and I managed to buy two blankets from them.

As we drove on, we saw giraffes wandering along the side of the road and further on we saw a Maasai shepard's goat get hit by a car. I guessed that both instances were just a daily part of Tanzanian life.

***

The following morning I woke up and went into Arusha. I was still pinching myself from the excitement of the day before and from seeing all the amazing creatures at the Crater. It had been such a great few days in Tanzania. My mission of the day was to try some local food. Tanzania's unofficial national dish is ugali (maize meal) and mishikaki (marinated meat kebabs) washed down with the local Safari or Kilimanjaro beer. Kilimanjaro's slogan was, "If you can't climb it, drink it", which I thought was pure brilliance.

Arriving in Arusha, I avoided the market where I knew that I would be hassled and instead spent the rest of the day at a local café, sipping African coffee and eating beans and ugali for lunch. The woman in the shop who sold it to me was surprised when I ordered it and gave me some free cabbage with it. I guessed she just couldn't believe a *mzungu* would eat such a traditional African meal.

Chapter Thirteen

"Kilimanjaro"

On the last day in Arusha, we were visiting a Maasai village. Our guide was a Maasai and would be telling us about the Maasai culture and way of life. Our first visit was to the Maasai Culture Museum, where various scenes of Maasai life with life-sized mannequins were set up. Maasai people still practiced circumcision on boys aged 14 and up. It was a ritual that meant adulthood. After the male circumcision ritual, everyone in the village would celebrate by getting drunk off of a local brew of honey beer that they made themselves. When the men had been circumcised, they would paint their faces with white dots which symbolized their journey to manhood. I had seen a few young men with faces painted white walking down the road on the way to the Ngorongoro

Crater. It was really interesting to see them still practicing their traditions. Female circumcision had also been a common ritual but it had now been banned in Tanzania. In female circumcision the woman was given no medication. So they were trying to cut down on it. I hoped that they could eliminate it, but I was sure that it was still going on in some places.

The Maasai man told us that the Maasai women typically built the huts and then men looked after the herd of goats or cows. They typically did not hunt. A man's wealth depended on how many cattle or goats he had, and when it came to marriage, the men had to pay the dowry with cows. The prettier the woman, the more cows her family would receive as a part of the wedding package. A beautiful woman could earn up to fifteen cows for her father. The families arranged the first marriage between the couple but the man could choose for himself when it came to additional wives.

The huts were surrounded by a fence of tangled acacia tree branches as they had sharp thorns that could protect the home's inhabitants from lion attacks (lion attacks!). The men had multiple wives so for example, a poor man might have ten wives and a rich man might have forty wives. Some villages were all made up of one family consisting of one man, his many wives, and all of their children. The village that we would be visiting that day was one of those. This time though, it was going to be the village of a poor man, with only ten wives and all of their children. The guide explained that the husband and wife slept separately, and the wife slept with the children.

He explained the Maasai diet next, the diet of milk and blood. He explained the blood had many nutrients and they usually cut the neck of a cow, but only a small cut so that they could only take a bit of blood at a time. They didn't have to kill the cow or anything like that. Still, I wouldn't like to be the cow of the Maasai, it would be the worst thing ever. Also, the Maasai branded the cows by making a cut along the sides, which ended up as a scar. The whole topic made me feel really sick and I was glad when it was over after someone asked if cow blood tasted good.

The guide explained that the clothes of the Maasai depended on what age and of course, what gender you were. The women wore long earrings which hung from big holes in their ears, not for any particular reason but just for fashion. However, married women wore special earrings in another style to show they were married. The jewelry was ornate and bold.

The guide said that when the Maasai people got sick, they would treat themselves with herbal concoctions made from local plants such as the acacia trees. They even had a concoction for malaria. I wondered if it worked or at least helped.

The Maasai did fight with other tribes of people and the guide showed us some of the spears and armor they used. They made calabashes to carry water and milk while moving around. He also explained that the Maasai people only lived in Tanzania and Kenya and they could wander freely into Kenya without having to do any kind of immigration checks. All in all, it was a really interesting talk.

After leaving the museum, the guide directed us to the village. It was a fair distance and we passed a couple of camels and donkeys on the way there. One of the donkeys had only three legs but I was happy to see he had still been kept around. Kids waved to us from houses and I saw women chopping down big thick bunches of tall grass, which were then put into bundles and strapped to a donkey's back to be carried somewhere. Even before we arrived at the village, we were greeted by the children of that village, who took our hands and wanted us to swing them up and down (requiring two people). Once they had us doing this, they absolutely couldn't get enough. They laughed and screamed and begged for more. They were curious about everything, our jewelry, watches, cameras, clothes. They wanted to try on our sunglasses and hats and it was really cute to see a pair of oversized sunglasses on a five year old girl's face. I got a close up shot of the same girl wearing a pair of someone's Ray-Ban's and the way the picture turned out, it could have been an advertisement for the brand.

There must have been about thirty kids in total, all with the same father. The mothers tended to stay in their own huts and I didn't really see them. The kids were all over us and they wanted us to take pictures of them and then see the picture afterwards. They absolutely loved it.

After playing with the kids, we followed the guide into one of the huts for a look inside. It was simple, built out of clay, with a thatched roof. We sat in some cow hide chairs according to age (the Maasai way, with the oldest getting the most respect, of course). I took a picture with one of the girls and then she asked me for money afterwards. We had been told that our fee covered taking pictures at the village so I politely told her I didn't have any. With all the kids surrounding me, it wasn't fair to give money to one and not the rest. I felt if I reached into my wallet it was just asking for trouble. On our way out, I noticed a little boy was playing with an old syringe. When he saw me, he pointed it at me and pretended to shoot me with it. I decided it was time to leave. Other than that, the kids were absolutely adorable.

Our next stop was at the Maasai clinic where the majority of patients had been bitten by snakes. There were four patients lying on beds, including one child who had been bitten by a cobra. It was horrible to see their limbs all bandaged up. Luckily, the clinic was free to them and was paid for by proceeds from the bar at the camp and also from our fees for the Maasai village walk. I hoped the patients would get better soon.

After the walk was finished, we had to leave for Marangu, the gateway to the towering Kilimanjaro Mountain, the highest mountain in Africa and the highest free-standing mountain in the world. Perhaps the most striking thing about Kilimanjaro was this very reason, that it was free-standing. It was something that just seemed to rise out of nowhere.

We stopped in Arusha to pick up supplies on the way out. Outside the supermarket, a man approached me, clicking his tongue. In some African languages, the click was actually a word or sound within a word. He held out a paper that said, "Please help Mr. X buy a new hearing aid". I apologized and walked away.

A few hours later, coming into Marangu, the scenery had changed drastically. I could see that it was now lush and tropical, with banana trees and tropical forests. The air was moist and there were tea and coffee plantations around. People waved and shouted "Jambo!" from the side of the road. I really liked it when I could change a person's frown to a smile, simply by waving to them from the truck. Kilimanjaro, at 5896m, rose in the distance, its top covered by a thick layer of mist. I could only make out the brown, lunar-like ridges on the bottom of the

144

volcanic mountain as it rose into the sky. At the campsite, I could even see it from my tent.

***

The next day was a free day and I decided to get out and take advantage of the warm weather, which meant heading into Marangu to get some lunch. I had been warned that there were a lot of hustlers and hasslers in town and to watch out. It didn't help that outside the camp, there was a group of men just hanging around waiting to "assist" any tourist leaving the camp, which meant they wanted to act as their "unofficial" guide.

I managed to play it cool with the guys outside however and lied to them to say I was meeting some friends for lunch. However, as soon as I got into town, another guy soon followed me and asked me what I was doing and where I was going. There was a system, I soon figured out. The guys would try and latch onto tourists and try to act like they had introduced us to a restaurant. They would then give us a price for the food (which was double the price the restaurant was actually charging) and make us pay them. They might give half to the restaurant and keep the other half to themselves. Regardless, I didn't see these guys hassling any of the locals. At one restaurant, I was told one price for the food by the staff, and then a price that was double that by the hustlers. I told the restaurant to forget the order and that I was leaving. I wasn't going to play around like that and have someone literally hanging out behind me and watching me the entire time I was eating.

Unfortunately, it was no different at the next place. Or the place after that. A man would attach himself to me and then try and tell me different prices for the food. In the end I just gave up as I was sick of being hustled. So I walked back to camp and sadly ate an avocado with crackers. At least I ate in peace.

Chapter Fourteen

"Doing the Hustle"

I headed to the market the first thing the next morning. It had been closed on the previous day because it was Sunday. People weren't hustling me nearly as bad as the previous day, probably because it was Monday, there were more shops open and more people working. The day was really clear and I could see the brown rocky top of Kilimanjaro jutting into the bright blue sky.

Once I got into town however, there were a few usual suspects trying to follow the group of us and "show" us the way. Our tour leader had told us to just tell them firmly that we didn't need any help and that we would probably have to say that several times to get the message across. Sure enough, after repeating the words several times, eventually, the "followers" would leave us alone. Although one did ask for breakfast instead, a clever tactic, I must admit.

The market was just opening up as we got into town and women wrapped in colorful sarongs and matching head scarves were setting up their wares to sell. The older women were busty and big-bottomed. Things for sale at the market ranged from second-hand socks to colorful fabric to fruits like custard apples, lime oranges, and passion fruit.

I wanted to buy some traditional African fabric, so made my way to the first fabric shop that I could make out. Of course, a hustler automatically stepped in front of me and pretended the shop was owned by him, which of course, it wasn't. I wondered if these people were a part of a gang who ran the town and who made the shop keepers charge a certain price for foreigners and then the hustlers got the extra money. I told him I didn't need anything and picked out a piece of multicolored fabric with red, yellow, and black flowers. I asked the woman who was actually running the shop how much it was and she quoted me double the price that I had been told the fabric cost. The reason for that is because the man hung around whispering prices and making comments, basically bullying her into selling me the fabric at a much higher price. I tried to bargain down but the man wouldn't have it so I left. I waited near the shop until the man left and then went back in and bargained with the woman again. This time she was more willing to talk about prices and so I ended up with a small wallet and a piece of fabric for a reasonable price. I told the woman not to give any money to the bullying hustler and she laughed.

I headed back as we were leaving soon to head to a campsite that was somewhere in between Kilimanjaro and Dar Es Saalam. Once on the truck, it was amazing to see the scenery change from lush and tropical at the foot of Kilimanjaro to a dry, dusty desert of red dirt and dry rocky-looking mountains. It reminded me of the desert in Nevada or Arizona in the U.S. Mud huts occasionally dotted the landscape and we pulled over to buy some firewood. One of the girls gave a child a banana from the truck and then we were told strictly by the tour leaders that we shouldn't give anything to anyone from the truck, otherwise we could be swarmed by people wanting things. The driver had once given a bag of lollipops to a few younger children and then proceeded to watch bigger kids come over and beat up the smaller ones to get the lollipops.

We also stopped at a fruit stand where I tried a custard apple for the first time. It was delicious and creamy and tasted just like it sounded. The only bad part was that it had huge black seeds in it that you had to either eat around or spit out. I bought an avocado from a guy who tried to sell it to me for double the price in the supermarket.

"But it's only 700 shillings in the supermarket, not 1,500 shillings," I protested.

"Okay, okay, 700," he agreed but then changed his mind and wanted me to buy a lime orange with the avocado for a smooth 1000 which I thought was fair enough.

The people at this little stand seemed happy to have us stop there. We had probably made their day simply because they were located in the middle of the desert and probably didn't get too much business.

We arrived at a simple campsite around dinnertime, where the only facilities available were in two rooms that the company had rented, just for us to use the toilets. The campsite had way too many insects, ranging from particularly nasty mosquitoes to millipedes the length of my forearm. In fact, I had

never quite been bitten by so many mosquitoes.

Needless to say, it was a long itchy night.

Chapter Fifteen

"An Island in the Sun"

I woke up still itching from all the insects in the tent. It was going to be a long drive into Dar es Saalam but I was looking forward to going to Zanzibar the following day. Powder sand and blue water beaches were waiting for me there.

We arrived in the late afternoon into Dar es Salaam, Tanzania's capital, with a population of about 2.5 million people. It was rumored to be an intriguing mix of African, Arabic and Indian influences. Its name meant "Haven of Peace" and was named so in the 1860s by Sultan Sayyid Majid of Zanzibar when he developed the area into a port and trading center.

We arrived at around 4 P.M. into our Dar es Salaam camp which was located right on the beach. It was beautiful and was the best campsite we had stayed at so far, with access to a beautiful blue Indian Ocean beach, a beach bar with Wi-Fi, Konyagi (a Tanzanian citrus spirit) gin slushes that were delicious and refreshing, and outdoor showers. The outdoor showers were each guarded by a secluded fence and had plenty of room. The water that came out however was only salt water but I didn't really care. The amazing part was just that showering under the palm trees in the warm breeze to the sound of ocean waves was incredible. The outdoor showers convinced me that someday, I would want to have one myself.

There was enough time for an early afternoon swim. The Indian Ocean at Dar es Saalam was an aquamarine color and was as warm as bathwater. African teenagers were also swimming in the ocean and they paid particular attention to the Caucasian girls. In fact, they swam around us in a circle, edging closer and closer. It was not an ominous feeling, just a feeling that they were curious about us.

The swim was perfect after a long and sweaty day sitting in the hot truck. The beach was what I had been waiting for. After I finished, I dried off and sat at the bar with a Konyagi slush while I checked my email. Mexican music played overhead and I was taken back to Cabo San Lucas, Mexico where I had spent one spring break during college happily sipping frozen margaritas with my friends in the hot sun. Ahh, Mexico…beach, sun, margaritas. Wait! What was I thinking? I was going to Zanzibar and drinking a Konyagi slush. There was nothing to think about but to enjoy the present moment. I would have happily spent a couple of days at this particular campsite but alas, it was only one night before we were off to Zanzibar in the morning.

My tour leader informed me that if I was happy with the beach at Dar es Salaam, then I would be ecstatic with the beach in Zanzibar. Fabulous.

***

The next morning we woke up early and piled into tuk-tuks that would take us from the campsite to the ferry terminal. The tuk-tuks were a reminder of traveling in Southeast Asia. We went through the rush hour of Dar es Salaam and got temporarily held up at a roadblock. It actually made me pretty nervous to be caught in such a crowd, especially as there was a fight among a group up ahead. I felt really vulnerable in the crowd, with all my bags, passport, and money within grabbing reach. I kept one arm looped through all my stuff while definitely being eyed by a few men looking at both me and my stuff. A guy came toward us, waving his arms wildly and grunting loudly. I had a small heart attack before I realized he was mute. Our driver gave him some money and he ran off and returned minutes later with a small piece of paper that looked like a certificate to give to the driver. Then he moved onto the next tuk-tuk driver, waving his arms wildly and grunting like a pig. That tuk-tuk driver punched the guy. I was assuming that he didn't know he was mute until too late, like I had done myself. Our driver obviously knew the guy so he hadn't appeared threatening to him. But if you didn't know he had a problem, he looked very threatening with his actions.

We left the guy behind when the roadblock was suddenly cleared and we were able to move onto the ferry. The ferry would take us across the channel to the other side of the city. It was clearly the morning rush, with veiled women on cell phones, and Muslim

African men with their beaded caps on their heads all rushing to squeeze on. With cars joining us as well, the ferry was officially packed. I hoped it wouldn't sink. Tanzania was definitely more Muslim than the other African countries I had been to so far and this was especially clear to see in the clothing of those on the ferry. Women wore long dresses, some plain black, others brightly-colored with matching veils.

Luckily we made it safely across to the other side and zoomed off the ferry in the tuk-tuk. We were the first among the tuk-tuks to reach the ferry terminal. We boarded the ferry, named Kilimanjaro 2, and were soon off, floating through the aquamarine sea. Fisherman on dhows (long, traditional fishing boats with sails) lined the sides of the channel, all trying to reel in the catch of the day with large nets. Some of the dhows looked ancient with their wind-battered sails. The sun shone with an intense fierceness and the reflection glinted off the water with a metallic glare.

We all sat upstairs on the top deck to see the view. The water was a beautiful lapis lazuli color. It took about three hours before we finally began to see what looked like Zanzibar, that legendary island that was commonly referred to as the "spice islands". Arabic-influenced buildings that had been worn over time with wind and rain greeted us at the harbor.

After going through immigration on Zanzibar, we piled into a minivan. Our guide on the island was a man named Ali, who was extremely laid back and easygoing. In fact, everyone on Zanzibar seemed to walk and talk just a *little* bit slower. We had entered island time, which moved at a pace behind the already slow pace of the mainland. Zanzibari women were all clothed in headscarves and almost everyone I saw was dressed in traditional Muslim clothing. Some of

the women were wearing a *kanga*, which was a
printed cotton wraparound skirt and some of the men
were wearing a *kikoi*, a printed cotton wraparound for
men. Zanzibar had a unique mix of people in its
history. It had been settled by the Persians, then the
Portuguese, and then the Omanis. Therefore, the
architecture and culture mostly reflected an Arabic
influence.

We stopped in the UNESCO world heritage
site of Stone Town to grab a snack of meat samosas
before setting off for Ningwe, the beach community
that we would be staying at for the next three nights
before returning to Stone Town. I couldn't wait to try
the spiced coffee in Stone Town, walk through the
Darajani market, and visit the old slave market near
the Anglican cathedral. Or visit the childhood home
of legendary rock star of the music group Queen,
Freddie Mercury, as he was originally from Zanzibar.

Once we had left Stone Town, we drove through lush palm fields and past throngs of schoolgirls clad in long skirts and pristine white veils. I caught a glimpse of aquamarine blue in between passing palm forests, a flash of the sea. People lived in mud brick houses and there were lots of bananas being sold from roadside stands. We reached Nungwe an hour after we set off, but it was an hour well worth waiting for. The beach was powder white sand and the water was crystal clear. It looked like an endless expanse of swimming pool water dotted with dhows here and there. What I had been waiting for had finally arrived. It was absolute paradise and one of the most beautiful beaches I had ever seen. I couldn't wait to get into the water. After everyone had checked into their rooms, we decided to grab a bite to eat at the adjoining restaurant to the Paradise Bungalows, where everyone was staying.

The first thing I learned over lunch was that "grabbing a bite to eat" did not exist in Zanzibar. One took things slowly, and that included eating. Again, this was the perfect example of *pole-pole*. I took a deep breath. *Slowly, slowly*. There was a saying in Tanzania in Swahili that went, "*Haraka, haraka, haina, baraka*" which meant "hurrying does not bring blessing".

The omelet and fries I ordered took somewhere between an hour and an hour and a half to arrive. By the time I had eaten and changed into my swimsuit, it was late afternoon. Still enough time for a swim in the perfect water. The sun was intense, and we had been warned by Ali to always wear sunscreen. He also said that most Zanzibarians only ate one meal a day because it was too hot. Something about the heat made people expand. Personally, I thought it was just because people didn't want to wait an hour and a half for every meal to be made.

I lay in the sun for about forty minutes while trying to fend off people who wanted to sell shell necklaces, artwork, etc. I could barely get five minutes of peace. More vendors came by, women offering hair braiding and henna tattoo services, and I told them I wasn't interested at the moment and they asked me when I *would* be interested. I decided this was perfect practice to hone my patience and tried to send out waves of positive energy into the world and peaceful vibes. It didn't work and I was soon frustrated again. It wasn't long before I ran into the ocean just to escape.

After a quick swim and lying out for a little bit, it was time to start getting ready for dinner. I took a cold shower and then headed down the beach, where the rest of the group was at Mungi's bar. The set up with the beach bars and restaurants was similar to Koh Samui, Thailand with tables on the beach and bars opening right out onto the shoreline. Mungi's bar was a typical beach bar and was pretty busy. There was a mix of both Westerners and Africans at the bar and although it was packed, the atmosphere was relaxed, as only a beach bar can be.

After a few drinks at Mungi's, the group of us followed an African Rastafarian down the beach who claimed there was a big party at a bar further down. However, when we arrived at his reggae bar, there was no one else there besides a few of his friends. We were, in fact, the party. They turned up the reggae music and we ordered a few Safari beers and danced to the music.

"I am Ugandan," the Rastafarian guy shouted over the music. "My father is from Uganda but I have never been there and was not been born there. We

Africans take the nationality of our fathers. My father

is Christian and my mother is Muslim. But I am a

Rasta."

Chapter Sixteen

"Zanzibarian"

I was going to swim with the sea turtles. After a morning of massages ($15 for one hour!), I set out with a few others and a guide to swim with the turtles. The guide showed us through the local village with its mud brick houses that had turned white in the intense sun. Women with colorful veils sat in doorways, chatting. Various head scarves and sarongs hung out to dry at houses and kids yelled hello. Shiny silver sardines glinted in the sharp sunlight on blankets, laid out to dry. We passed a fish market closer to the aquamarine sea where the catch of the day was arranged on plastic tarps on the sand. Wooden dhows bobbed in the turquoise sea and they were also being made near the beach. Kids played soccer and little girls walked back from school in their school uniforms of white veils and long blue dresses.

One group of guys took a picture of one of the girls in the group, but the picture was of her knees. In these African Muslim countries, we had been warned as women to cover our shoulders and knees anywhere we went in public. This was out of respect for the Muslim way of dressing, as the local women also did not show their shoulders or knees and remained covered up. The only problem with this was that it was so hot. So when the guy took a picture of the girl's knees, it was kind of comical. Perhaps to them it was almost like getting a flash of cleavage. What was exotic to some was mind boggling.

The sun was shining brightly and the sea looked gorgeous as we walked along the powdery sand. We continued through a small group of palm trees until we reached a natural lagoon. There were about six large sea turtles swimming around in a pool of other fish and about four smaller sea turtles. We walked down to the edge of the pool. There was a huge turtle, the biggest I had ever seen, with large black eyes and gray flippers. We were allowed to feed the turtles from a bucket of bright green dried seaweed, the same seaweed that I had seen washed up on the seashore. There were also huge fish in the lagoon, grey-colored with huge black eyes in addition to smaller zebra-striped fish.

I eased myself in, getting used to the turtles by feeding them first. The bigger ones of course pushed the smaller ones out of the way to get to the food, so I tried to throw some to the smaller ones. While I fed the large ones, I tentatively touched them. Usually I didn't have any problem with touching reptiles, etc. but somehow, turtles give me the creeps. But I pet their great big heads, which were as hard as their shells. The flippers were also hard as their shells. The only thing that was soft was their necks, which was like putting your finger into soft tofu. In fact, it was extremely soft and mushy. This only confirmed that I still thought turtles were kind of creepy.

After I had thoroughly touched the turtles, I put on a snorkel mask and eased myself into the clear lagoon. The fish darted around me nervously and the turtles swam everywhere, they didn't seem bothered. The turtles swam at me and I made a hasty retreat to the edge of the pool. The largest turtle in the pool was about 30 years-old. They could live until 120 years old so the 30 year-old was actually quite young. I was surprised at how much they ate; even a bucket of seaweed didn't seem to slow them down.

Swimming with the turtles was a fun experience and I was glad I had done it. We walked back to the Paradise Bungalows along the gorgeous white powder beach. More vendors stopped us along the way. The excuse that I thought worked the best with them was to say that I was going to meet friends for a bite to eat, so didn't have time to stop and look at anything they were selling. The only time this didn't work was when they wanted to lead me to a restaurant of their friend's, uncle's, etc.

For dinner, I was meeting everyone at the restaurant next door to the Paradise Bungalows, called Langi Langi, which was rumored to have the best food in Zanzibar. Once I had showered and dressed and arrived at Langi Langi, I was starving and ready for this amazing meal. I ordered a spinach and green bean masala curry with Zanzibar spices. It came with a starter of potato and leek soup with a homemade bread roll. The ambiance was so gorgeous, with a patio overlooking the ocean and the star-studded night sky. Candles flickered all around and mostly couples dined on the quaint wooden tables.

My masala was absolutely delicious and was accompanied by Zanzibar potatoes which had a kind of spicy creamy mayonnaise on them. I do believe that the masala was the best I have ever had in my entire life.

***

The next morning I woke up feeling great. It was the first day on the entire trip that I hadn't booked anything and there were no plans to do anything. I had a leisurely breakfast and read the newspaper that I had stuffed in my bag and never had a chance to read. After breakfast, I made my way to the Hilton for a swim in their pool. Some of the group were staying at the Hilton and had openly invited everyone to come and swim in the pool and use the Wi-Fi freely. So I decided that Hilton, it was. The pool was lovely and was not shockingly cold which was nice. I lay on the lounge chair for a while and had swims intermittently. At the Hilton I was also invited to do a water aerobics class, even though I wasn't actually staying there (although I don't think anyone noticed or cared). The instructor taught us an African song and we sang it as we did some aerobics in the water. I had slathered myself with sunscreen before but I was pretty sure that it had washed off in the pool (although it said water resistant) because later, when I came back to the Paradise Bungalows, I was bright red. That wasn't even the start of it.

Once back at the Paradise Bungalows, I had another massage, although this time I really shouldn't have since I was freshly burned. Some sand on my skin got caught up in the massage oil and scraped against my freshly burned and tender skin. I should have told the masseuse to stop but stupidly bit my lip and remained silent.

After the massage, I didn't feel too hot and went to take a cold swim in the ocean. It really was like a swimming pool, the water was so clear. After my swim, I went back to the room and lay on the bed, generally feeling like death on a stick. I was pretty sure I had heat exhaustion. Even too much of a good thing could be bad.

***

The next morning we were off to Stone Town, a UNESCO World Heritage site. It was about an hour from Nungwe where we were staying. We were picked up in a minivan and after passing through villages and small markets on the side of the road, tropical palm forests, and roadblocks, we arrived in Stone Town at the Karibu Inn. "Karibu" meant "welcome" in Swahili and we heard it every time we entered a shop.

Karibu Inn was located in the heart of Stone Town and although it wasn't flashy, it would do for the night. It was definitely a step up from camping even though the room slightly resembled a prison cell. There was also a cat in the room, strangely enough. I let it out though because I eventually realized that it wasn't going to let me pet it. I mean, what's the use of a cat if it won't even let you pet it? The staff at the Inn were certainly less than friendly, but there wasn't much that could be done about it.

I set out for Stone Town, which was made up of a series of winding streets that were very narrow with old, weather-worn buildings in an Arabic-style adorned with stunningly-carved wooden doors in accents of gold and with recessed inner courtyards. Next to them were Indian-influenced buildings designed with ornate balconies and latticework and the streets were bustling with activity. I can imagine that Stone Town was the closest to something you would see in a Moroccan or Tunisian market town. There was a multitude of shops selling handmade woven bags, harem pants in a variety of designs and colors, beaded earrings, animal-print wooden bracelets, tropical-print dresses, wooden carvings, bowls, etc. I was overwhelmed at first because there were so many vendors saying "please come into my shop, etc." It was like they knew I was fresh meat and they were ready to prey on me. I *did* discover that the shops that were closer to the Main Street seemed to be pricier than the shops that were pushed way back. Perhaps not as many tourists reached that spot.

The day was cloudy and the air smelled of rain. It wasn't long before I got caught in a torrential downpour that stopped all activity while people paused in doorways until the rain ebbed. The streets were quickly flooded with about five inches of water which moved downwards like a rushing stream.

After the rain died off, I looked for somewhere to eat but there didn't seem to be any restaurants tucked away into the back streets, they were mostly coffee houses selling the famous spiced Zanzibarian coffee. I found a woman selling scarves and harem pants who managed to get me inside of her shop. The woman had a little daughter asleep on the floor and pleaded with me to buy something so she could buy milk for her baby. The child was dressed very cutely and didn't seem to be starving or have any health problems so I was sure it was just a tout to get more money. Unfortunately when people mention babies it pulls on my heart strings and I can't resist. So, I ended up buying a pair of elephant-print, black and white harem pants for around 10 dollars. Later when I tried to find the woman again to buy some scarves from her, the shop seemed to have disappeared and I couldn't find it again.

I walked past the old fort walls, now yellow and streaked with black from age and weather and made my way back to the seafront where I had seen some good Indian restaurants. There was a mix of people on Zanzibar, mostly African Muslims but also some Middle Eastern and Indian people. I stopped at an Indian restaurant where I had a channa masala (chickpea curry) and rice, along with my Coke. I never drank Coke at home that much but when traveling, it was essential to drink it with meals because I swore it prevented against getting food poisoning. The food was delicious and the chef himself came out to ask if it was alright.

After lunch I walked to the House of Wonders, Zanzibar's National Museum, which held some Swahili cultural relics and some history on Zanzibar. A German man stood outside, trying to sell a book that showed different photographs of Zanzibar for $22. He must have lived in Zanzibar if he was doing that. I felt a bit sorry for him as no one was going to buy that book for $22.

Next, it was a stroll along the Forodhani Gardens, along the seafront where fishing boats were coming in with their catches of the day. While walking, two different men at various times asked me to visit their stall at the night market. In fact, they seemed to pop up at different places throughout the afternoon, making sure that I would visit their stall at the night market. One of them called himself Mr.

Bean and asked for my empty plastic bottle that had once held some water in it. I asked him if he was going to recycle it and he said no, he was going to give it to his mother who would make juice and store it in that container.

I walked through the winding streets some more and ended up at Freddy Mercury's former childhood house. The lead singer of Queen had indeed been born in Zanzibar to Persian parents from India who had emigrated from India to Zanzibar. They eventually fled due to political unrest and settled in England. The rest is history.

After a quick look at the Mercury house, I went for a spiced coffee, which came black and really *was* spicy. It tasted like they put ginger, cinnamon, and cloves in the coffee and it made my throat tingle. As I drank my coffee, another downpour of rain fell outside. After it ebbed, it was back to the hotel for a shower and a change of clothes.

The night market started at 6:30 and I arrived there just as it started. Immediately, one of the men I had seen all afternoon spotted me and sent me to his stall. There was really no getting out of it.

"Come, come, come with me," he said, pointing to his stall and hurrying me along.

I was going to have to buy something in order for him to leave me alone. The night market was actually a food market, with skewers of blue marlin, kingfish, mussels, lobster, scallops, shrimp, etc. In addition to seafood, there were grilled sweet potatoes, cassava, breadfruit, falafel, green bananas, plantains, etc. The prices were extremely expensive.

"I'm a vegetarian," I lied to the vendor because I only wanted a falafel and a piece of breadfruit.

I had never tried breadfruit before. I bargained with him on the price and he said a higher price but I got him down to 5,000 shillings for one piece of breadfruit and a falafel which was about four dollars. Neither was very good, the falafel was dry and tasted like cold bread with no flavor and the breadfruit was bland except for some salt that had been poured on it. The breadfruit reminded me of potato, especially with the salt.

While I was eating, a man came over to "talk" to me.

"I am so poor, I have no money," he said. "I don't have any money for food."

"Do you want the rest of my food?" I asked him, offering him the plate.

He grabbed the plate from me and yelled out, "How is this supposed to feed my five kids?"

No please, no thank you. So I simply got up and walked away. This was begging gone wild and I didn't want to have anything to do with it. The man was dressed relatively well, had no apparent health problems, did not appear starving, and I was sure that he wasn't as poor as he made himself out to be. But he obviously made money from his gimmick at the night market.

He stood up to plead with me for some money. I escaped him when I went to buy a Coke from another man who told me that the guy pestering me was nicknamed "Mr. Disturbance". He recommended me to just tell him that I was trying to enjoy my vacation in peace and to please leave me alone. It was certainly easier said than done.

It wasn't long before I was spotted by Mr. Bean who led me to his stand next. I was full and didn't want any more so I bought some coconut bread

for 2000 shillings (about $1.50). It was a piece of
grilled flatbread that didn't even taste like coconut.
Mr. Bean looked pretty disappointed that I didn't
spend much money but at least he was off my back
for now. I snuck out of the night market before I
could get hassled again.

Chapter Seventeen

"A Journey Ahead"

The next morning was a rough one; we had to be up at 5 A.M. for breakfast and then had to be at the ferry port by 6:15 A.M. to catch the 7 A.M. ferry. The morning went by in a groggy rush and even the ferry ride seemed shorter (although it always does when you are leaving your holiday destination to go "home"). The ferry ride going back to Dar es Salaam was pretty bumpy, but I had taken some anti-motion sickness pills so I was okay although others were throwing up. The ride was beautiful, with sightings of dolphins and a beautiful rainbow that stretched over the ocean, both endings visible.

Back in Dar es Salaam, we passed a bustling fish market, bursting with people, and our tour leader bought us a tuna from the market which we would cook later. But for now, it was time to get back on the road again. We stopped off at a shopping center to get some supplies. My sunburn from Zanzibar was killing me but the aloe vera sun gel in the pharmacy was way too expensive so I just slathered myself with body lotion.

After the stop, we piled back on the truck. I had discovered that my feet were swollen and I could no longer see my ankles. My legs were covered in prickly heat and I had blisters forming on my shoulders and tops of my thighs. In fact, my legs felt tight and swollen everywhere, most likely from a combination of sitting down all day in the truck, sunburn, and dehydration. I drank so much water that I had to use the restroom twice during the night. It was only then that I realized that I rarely went to the restroom. I wasn't drinking enough water. It definitely wasn't good but somehow along the way I had developed the idea that going to the restroom was bothersome and had consequently stopped drinking water.

On the road again, the scenery of Tanzania was ever so changing and this time it was of rocky boulders that were in such large piles that they had become large rocky hills. The hills were lumpy with gray boulders jutting out. There was even one advertisement on a huge boulder; what a great way to use natural resources. Trees were sparse and the sun was so intense that I was sure any white person would burn in half an hour of sitting in it. Cloud shadows played on the landscape, constantly shape shifting. Brown, mud brick huts dotted the dusty, beige land. Some huts had straw-thatched roofs; some huts had fences of sticks jutting out of the ground. The huts blended in with the dry land. I saw outlines of gardens etched in the dry earth with nothing growing, as water must have been sparse. The cluster of huts reminded me of a Native American settlement of adobe houses. Kids pointed at us and adults stopped mid-conversation to look at a truck full of *mzungus*.

We passed an old woman with cloudy eyes stooped in her doorway. She was a rare sight in Africa because the local life expectancy is so low. Forty was old here. Kids waved from the road and walked hand in hand. Some smiled and gave the thumbs up sign. Makeshift mosques with a half moon and star figure on the top peered out from the rooftops of small villages. Little boys walked besides small herds of African cattle, looking very grown up with their long walking sticks. We passed a shirtless man making bricks in an outdoor oven. Goats and cows grazed on dead grass side by side, their heads to the ground.

In the late afternoon we found ourselves in Mikuni National Park on our way to the campsite. At sunset, I saw giraffes, zebra, gazelle, baboons, water buffalos, warthogs, and best of all, African elephants with long white tusks. It was a great way to end a long day.

Chapter Eighteen

"Goodbye Tanzania, Hello Malawi!"

I was sad to say goodbye to Tanzania, it had been a great place to see the Africa that I had always imagined, with all of its unique animals and its array of landscapes. The morning on the truck passed by uneventfully and after lunch we neared the border of Malawi. Stopping before the border, we all took the opportunity to change money from Tanzanian shillings to Malawian Kwacha with a man who called himself "Mr. Cool", about ten minutes before entering Malawi. I discovered at the border that his rate hadn't been so good. I had lost out on about 5 or 6 dollars from the exchange rate that the Foreign Exchange office was giving as opposed to Mr. Cool's.

Our tour leader told the women in our group to remain covered up (knees but not shoulders) as

Malawi had been very traditional and closed off from

outside influences for a while and therefore one had

to remain covered. For some reason, the heat seemed

to get more intense after we crossed the border.

Perhaps that's because I had to cover my knees and

shoulders. I hastily bought a can of locally produced

pineapple juice which on afterthought cost me almost

two dollars. At the time I was so hot and in need of a

cold drink I didn't care about bartering. The border

crossing was easy and I also didn't have to pay for a

visa this time which was wonderful.

Upon entering the "warm heart of Africa"

which was Malawi, I was happy to see that the

women had gone back to wearing African-print

headdresses and colorful sarongs, which seemed to

somehow be more like the sub-Saharan "African"

which lived up to my stereotype (even though I knew

it was partially incorrect due to the huge Muslim influence in the African people).

Malawi remains one of the world's poorest countries, with a per capita gross national product (GNP) of less than US$250. Nearly half the population is chronically malnourished and life expectancy is only 43 years due in large part to the HIV/AIDS infection rate in Malawi, which runs at almost 12%. Around half the population is under 15 years of age. This was also the first country where we would no longer be hearing Swahili, because the language in Malawi was Chichewa.

Despite those shocking statistics, Malawi was considered "Africa for beginners" due to being relatively safe to get around and the friendliness of the people. The first rule of thumb that I had seen in Africa with the people was that it was useless to get impatient over the slowness of life here. No one was in a hurry it seemed and as far as they were concerned, you shouldn't be either.

The first famous explorer to arrive to Malawi was the well-known Dr. David Livingstone, who reached Lake Malawi in 1859 and whose death inspired many to come after him, mostly in the form of missionaries. This is reflected in the fact that about 75% of the country is Christian. However, some of those Christian beliefs have been combined with local African beliefs forming a kind of fusion religion.

Once we had been on the road for a while in Malawi, the scenery seemed to change to a lush and tropical one, with flatlands of fields containing crops and veggie plants. Kids waved and jumped from the side of the road and some adults waved too. Healthy-looking Brahman cattle grazed on fields and brown mud brick one-room homes dotted the landscape, many with the familiar thatched rooftops.

I soon caught a glimpse of deep blue water in the distance, with the sun glinting off of it. It was Lake Malawi, of course, a huge lake that was so big, it looked like an ocean. Lake Malawi is the third largest lake in Africa and it has more fish species than any other inland body of water in the world, with a total of over 600. As we drove on, the lake revealed itself to us and it was gorgeous. I soon saw that this shimmering sea of water had a faint outline of mountains in the background and this must have been the other side of the lake. Passing by small villages situated on the lake, I saw thousands of dried silver fish laid in the sun and the stench filled the air momentarily. The fish were lined up on the shore, tended to by a couple of lucky fishermen. In the distance, I could see fishermen in canoes and small boats on the lake. This lake was their lifeline.

A large plateau loomed ahead, green and lush with the occasional red rocky outcrop peeking out. We arrived at Chitimba Camp not too long after and as we drove along the road to get to the camp, kids swarmed the road and ran alongside the truck, smiling and waving. They seemed truly happy to see us. There were a few vendors selling wood carvings outside of the camp and they yelled at us to have a look at their shop from the side of the road.

The campsite was in a perfect location, set right on the beach-like shores of Lake Malawi. It wasn't often I had a lake-side view.

Chapter Nineteen

"A Call to the Witchdoctor"

The next day I woke up to a beautiful view of Lake Malawi, with the early morning light dancing off the water. I had accidentally woken up with the sunrise that morning, groggily seeing through morning eyes a wash of pinks and oranges stretched over the sky above the lake.

A few kids played along the shore and the sun hung lazily in the sky. The air felt heavy with languid heat. I had decided that I was going to join some others from the group to visit the local witchdoctor. He would give us a prediction about our future and would also perform a ceremonial dance for us. We had hired a local guide to take us there and to show us the way.

At 10 A.M. we met the local guide, a short guy who was probably in his forties, and left the camp. We were immediately followed by a group of lanky young guys dressed in long shorts and t-shirts who had stalls selling wood carvings outside of the camp. Of course they wanted us to buy something from them but we had been told by our tour leaders not to buy from them as they tended to hassle people a lot. However, there was no way to get rid of them; they continued to follow us then and for the rest of the day. In addition to the vendors, we were followed by a few young kids from the village, who walked up to us, smiling, and simply latched onto our hands. They couldn't have been older than seven. It was the purest act of genuine sweetness that I had ever seen to come up to a stranger, acting like you had known them forever. I didn't know any other continent in the world whose children walked up to foreigners, smiled, wanted to hold their hands, and walk along with them. The kids of Africa were a definite highlight, most of them always smiling and waving and latching onto our hands. I had not seen a single child crying. Of course if you didn't like kids, it could be a nightmare, as they often wanted you to take a picture of them so they could see the image and also wanted to touch everything that was on you. They loved bracelets and jewelry in general and were curious about everything. They were like our little shadows, following us wherever we went.

We followed the guide through a small run-down village to the witchdoctor's house, which was located behind some squat concrete houses amongst a bunch of lush banana trees. We had now gathered about thirty of the neighborhood children with us, some of them orphans I was told. There were babies all the way to pre-teens. All the kids were carrying the babies and looking after them. The babies were tied to their hips in slings made from African-print material. Some of the babies looked so snug all wrapped up. Sometimes, only their heads poked out. They were usually quite calm and when they wanted to cry, they were usually passed from child to child. It was amazing to see all these little "babysitters", some of them not many years older than the babies themselves. Every one of the kids shared responsibilities to look after the babies of the village while the mothers were busy with house or farm work. And these kids were extremely well-behaved.

The kids huddled around us in a tight circle as we sat on Malawi-style woven mats on the ground. The witchdoctor's wife hobbled over first. She was perhaps in her sixties, carrying a kind of instrument that sounded like shaking bells. The witchdoctor himself followed, he looked quite old and lean, with long, tangled dreads. He had deep lines in his face and had painted it with white lines that made him look like he was going to war. Later I learned he was only in his fifties. He was wearing a red t-shirt with a cross that was similar to the Red Cross symbol and a matching pair of long, baggy red shorts. His ankles, wrists, and waist were wrapped with a string of handmade metal bells that jingled as he moved. He snorted something out of a pipe and looked like he was entering into some kind of trance. He began to dance wildly, hopping from foot to foot, to a song that was fueled by two men banging on bongo drums. This went along with a kind of whooping sound from his wife, along with the jangling of the strange instrument she carried. He shook with the music and seemed to be at one with it. His eyes were intense. He locked eyes with me as he danced and I felt almost scared, like I could not look away. He seemed to be in a trancelike state and I wasn't sure whether I was supposed to stare back and smile or break eye contact.

He danced for a while and I could tell when something was wrong with the beat because he would suddenly break out of his trance, looking agitated, and point his long wrinkled finger at whoever was not doing something correctly. Then, when the beat was to his liking again, he would smile and go back into a trancelike state. His face crinkled into a million lines when he smiled.

He began calling us up one by one to dance with him. The way he chose the person he wanted to dance with was by handing them a thick wooden stick with horse hair tied to the end of it. It was soon my turn. I think he was enjoying dancing with all the girls. After the dancing ended, he retreated into his one-room house. We were then to go in one by one to get a consultation with him.

The consultations took a while and as people came out, they said that he had predicted some accurate things. He told one of the girls that she had been educated in America which was true. He predicted to another girl that one of her relatives worked in the airline industry and that was how she could travel so much, which was also true. When it came to my turn, I was really nervous. In fact, I was shaky and felt slightly sick and I had no idea why. Perhaps I thought he was going to tell me something that was life-changing. Inside the hut, there was only me, the witchdoctor, and a translator. The room was dark, but there were voodoo dolls hanging up with pins stuck in them. This guy clearly dabbled in black magic. As I entered, the witchdoctor snorted something out of a pipe and then closed his eyes so he could see what visions he had of my future.

He mumbled something to the translator, who turned to me.

"You are still fresh and will be doing more traveling. Your family is strong and they are thinking of you here in Africa."

The witchdoctor paused, taking a shaky breath and gave me a glazed eyed smile.

"You will be married and have two children. They will be girls," the translator said. "You have also spent part of your time in one country and part of your time in another."

I nodded, for this was true.

The witch doctor snorted out of his pipe and mumbled a few words with closed eyes. I could see his eyeballs rolling back and forth underneath his eyelids.

"You are healthy and will live a long life. You have a mother, father, brother, and sister and said they are all healthy and well," the translator explained. "Your trip in Africa will go well. You will be back to Africa when you are older."

In comparison to the other consultations, mine had not been too specific but it was still interesting to hear him predict about my life. He had been doing the witchdoctor work for nine years and said that anyone could learn to do it. He saw the predictions in his dreams and when I looked closely, his eyelids were actually flickering so maybe he was dreaming while awake (or in a drug-induced trance).

I was really glad to see him perform his duties and as I waited for the others to finish, I played with the kids outside. There was one little girl who was so shy at first but as I spoke to her she warmed up to me a little and then began to hold my hand. She was absolutely adorable with big brown eyes, a shaved head, and wearing an African print skirt with no shirt.

She must have only been around four-years-old. After she had secured my hand, she wouldn't let it go and would cry out if another child tried to grab my hand. I played with her for some time and said "are you shy?" at which she simply responded and kept repeating, "shy, shy, shy..."

We stopped for lunch on the way back to camp at a local restaurant, which looked like the front room of someone's house, with a few plastic tables dotted about. The only thing that made it a restaurant was that someone had written the word, "*chakula*" on the outside of it, which meant "food" in Chichewa. We were the only customers and the owner looked quite pleased to see us all at once. I had beans and cooked cabbage with salty rice. It was delicious. After lunch, we went to the local market where I bought three bunches of gorgeous traditional African fabrics and a Malawian woven mat from a very friendly local man who laughed loudly every time I pointed to a piece of fabric and asked, "How much?" The fabric was the cheapest I had seen so far anywhere in Africa, only $3.50 cents for about two yards. The designs were varied and gorgeous, all energetic with bright colors and punchy patterns. I also couldn't believe that for the price of the mat, I paid about $1.70 and it was about seven feet long and four feet wide. It would be perfect as a yoga mat or a mat in the kitchen or patio. How I would get all of these things back home I had no idea but in the middle of my shopping extravaganza, I decided it was something that could be dealt with later.

The male vendors from the shops near the camp who had joined us from the beginning of the tour now tried even harder to sell us something, from carved key chains to necklaces with wooden giraffes hanging from them. I felt really bad for them as they were clearly desperate for a sale. I mean, they had followed us all day long in hopes that we would buy something from them. They also said that they were willing to trade some of their carvings for any clothes that we didn't want anymore.

"Please have a look sister," they said.

I really wished I had come to Africa with a huge bag of stuff. In Malawi, they would trade you a souvenir for some t-shirts or clothes, magazines or books. I was itching to go through my stuff to see what kind of things that I wanted to trade. I was sure I could come up with something.

Back at the campsite, I retreated to my tent. There were monkeys overhead, very cute ones by the looks of it. I climbed out of the tent to have a closer look. One of them seemed to be mocking me as I tilted my head to see it from a better angle. Sure enough, it was interested in my movements and came closer for another look. It appeared to want to jump on me so I moved back and around the corner. Better not to tease the monkeys, you never know what they will do.

Chapter Twenty

"Kande Beach"

The next morning we set out for Kande Beach, which was on the other side of Lake Malawi. We stopped in the small town of Mzuzu along the way for a chance to shop for the "bad taste" party that we were going to have the following night. We had been given a budget by our tour leaders and told to shop for horrible-looking clothes for a person whose name we had drawn out of a hat. It was comical because when we stopped to buy the clothes, the vendors had anticipated us and had an entire range of horrible clothes on hand to sell. To further define "horrible clothes", I mean pants with tails sewed into the back, silly Peter Pan-inspired skirts, tacky flower-print stockings, jester caps, wigs, eighties-style glittery jackets, etc. We had a budget of about five dollars to spend on the outfits and I gleefully picked out women's stockings, a shimmery pink Peter Pan skirt, a leopard-print top and jester-style bracelets.

Mzuzu had a huge second-hand clothes market, all of which were sourced from charities in the West. They were all the second-hand clothes donations from abroad. Basically, when the clothes were donated to Africa, they were separated into jeans, shirts, dresses and put into "bales" which were then sold to people who then sold them at clothes markets. So there was big business in second-hand clothes in Africa.

After shopping for all those horrible clothes, I stopped in the supermarket to pick up a few things, including batteries which I was shocked to see cost 7 dollars for four of them. Imported things were very expensive in Malawi. It looked like I wouldn't be buying batteries anytime soon, I only had four left but

I was too stubborn to pay 7 dollars for another pack of four. I stopped for lunch at a local cafe with Wi-Fi for a burger and fries, which to my dismay took an hour and a half to come out. Food service was so slow in Africa, it was better to not go to a restaurant starving because it was certain you would have to wait close to an hour to get your food. I was sure there were exceptions (I just hadn't found any yet). Again, getting impatient was useless here.

We were back on the road soon after lunch, traveling through winding canyons with lush green mountains on both sides of the road. We stopped at a wood market, where I bought some beautiful ebony bookends with an elephant and tail on them for about five dollars plus two

T-shirts that I traded. I also traded another T-shirt and a roll of toilet paper for a bracelet at another stall which was okay. It was fun to trade and I was sure that I could find some more stuff in my bag to trade with vendors. Trading stuff was so much fun. I just wished I had brought more.

We arrived at Kande Beach camp in early evening. It was absolutely beautiful, with a long stretch of golden sandy beach. Here, the lake really *did* look like the ocean, with waves and all. The water was a pretty color, a light blue on the shore and a deeper blue as you looked further out. There was a small island that appeared to be really close to shore but our tour leader said that people had drowned trying to swim to it, so not to attempt to do so. There was a nice canopy-top bar and a shaded area in which to camp.

The following day we were cooking a whole pig underground and having the bad taste party with our horrible clothes. I crawled into my tent early that night. The next day would be a long one.

***

The next morning, I watched the two African guys prepare the pig that was going to be roasted. It had just been killed that morning and the only thing that comforted me was that it had probably led a happier life than pigs that had grown up in factories that were enclosed in pens that were too small. I still felt bad for eating it though even though I wasn't a vegetarian. I was the kind of person who just didn't want to meet the cow before eating it if you know what I mean. The men had already gutted it and it was stretched out on a kind of grill. They salted it, rubbed some oil in it, and then put it over hot coals that had been put in a sand pit in the ground.

Later that night, we played some music and danced before the pig roast. The roast was delicious and we all literally "pigged" out. After that, the outfits

for the bad taste party were revealed. I ended up with

a very bright gold sparkly jacket, a glittery top, a kind

of child's playsuit, and a pink skirt. It looked hideous

but that's what it was all about. Outfits ranged from

people looking like they should be an extra in a Peter

Pan production to someone who stepped out of a 70s

disco club. The rest of the night was spent dancing the

night away at the bar. Two African ladies showed me

how to shake my body in the proper way and showed

me the Malawi way to dance. It was so much fun that

I forgot what I was wearing.

***

The next day was a free day and I couldn't

have been happier. The day was perfect, sunny and

warm with not a hint of cloud in the sky. The only

problem was that even by 7 A.M., the tent was absolutely steamy. I decided to go for a swim on the beautiful beach. The water could not have been a more perfect temperature and it was so clear that you could see the designs that the waves had made into the sand, and also glimpse small fish swimming around. I lay in the sun for a little bit and it felt so good and warm. I soon remembered my blistering skin from Zanzibar and tried not to stay in the sun for too long. My skin was now peeling off in sheets, it looked horrible. Everywhere was peeling, my shins, upper thighs, arms, chest, stomach, and shoulders. I hated to think of the damage that had been caused.

I was just about to lay down for a nap when I saw what looked like clouds of black smoke on the horizon, above the lake. But it wasn't actually smoke, it was large clouds of flies who had gathered above the lake to mate. There had been documentaries on this and I was seeing it firsthand. It really did look like huge black clouds of smoke and I hated to imagine how many flies were in those clouds. There were about five of them on the horizon and they were quickly moving closer. Everyone cleared the beach and went back to close up their tents in case the fly cloud landed on our part of the land. Luckily it didn't but they landed on both sides of us, further down the beach. I wondered if any fisherman had been caught in a fly cloud and winced at the horrible thought of it. We came out unscathed though. I was grateful for that.

Chapter Twenty-One

"Malawi to Mozambique"

Before I left Kande Beach the following day to head to Malawi's capital city, Lilongwe, I met an aid worker at the camp bar while I was getting a coffee. I had only happened to meet her because she was running late. Wherever she went in the village, she was always stopped by locals to chat and she said she could barely get anywhere anymore because she was always stopping and chatting with someone in the village who wanted to speak to her.

"I work with the poor in the local village. There is no work for them. I think 50% of them are below the poverty line. The men are lazy and don't have a good work ethic, the women are doing everything. They do the housework, they take care of the gardening, and the farm work."

There were also many people affected by HIV/AIDS and there were many orphans in the village whose parents had passed away from AIDS. Women in Malawi could legally get married at age 15 but some of them got married as young as 11 or 12. Therefore, there were a lot of cases of teen pregnancies and half of the population of Malawi (12 million) were under the age of 15.

The aid worker, whose name was Cecilia, said that there was one clinic in Kande Beach and it was a great one. However, it wasn't much use, as the local people couldn't even afford to eat, let alone purchase 50 Kwacha valued meds (about 15 cents). She also said it was frustrating because Links International, the Christian charity that supplied the clinic, wouldn't allow the clinic to distribute condoms freely to prevent HIV. Instead they promoted abstinence which didn't always work. However, there were countless organizations and groups like the Peace Corps doing wonderful things in Africa and really helping people. And I wished I could thank them for their services. It seemed like the organizations that were really helping were the ones that promoted education and skills for agriculture. The African governments had become reliant on Western aid for far too long and the same problems still existed. I thought back to the man in Uganda who spoke with me about micro-finance loans and how they should be going to people who were actually intending to start a business. I agreed that there should be a focus on agricultural education so that people could start feeding themselves better.

I could tell that Cecilia was burnt out from aid work. She had come to Africa hoping to see a real change.

"I have helped many people but it's time that the African people start to learn how to train for the positions that the aid workers are doing," she expressed to me.

With these thoughts on my mind, I hopped aboard the truck to head to Lilongwe. Along the way, the earth began to look dry and I didn't see any animals grazing off of the land like I had seen in other parts of Africa, although in this case, there wasn't much to graze on. In this part of Malawi, the land was flat and dry and trees grew sporadically. I wasn't sure how they survived in the intense heat. Mud brick buildings, the shade of caramel with thatched straw roofs, dotted the landscape. Shirtless kids ran around their yards and waved at us. Random flashes of bright orange flowering trees gave everything color. The sky was a pale blue and full of thin, wispy clouds. The air smelled like something was burning; it could have been the scorched earth.

***

The next day was a free day in Lilongwe but I wasn't ready for it. I had been up all night because my tent had been infested by ants. And not just some ants, but about a million ants. It seemed I had camped on top of an ant farm the size of New York. The ants attacked the tent in throngs, they were everywhere. And some of them bit. So after getting woken up by the ants, I moved my tent to another location and cleaned out the ants. The only problem was that there were so many ants that I couldn't have possibly gotten them all. So I didn't get much sleep, with ants crawling all over my skin. In fact, the sensation stayed with me all throughout the night and it wasn't nice.

So when I left with my tour leaders for town at about 8 A.M. I was feeling only half alive from two nights of no sleep. The tour leaders needed to go to town because we were going to Mozambique the following day and needed a visa to transit through. Unfortunately there was some power surge problem at the embassy so our visas were taking longer than expected and they needed to go pick them up. Needless to say I caught a ride into town with them because I really needed to change some money. After we arrived, I dragged myself to the bank and changed some money. What I needed was a stiff drink and a bed that was free of ants. The traditional beer of Malawi was made from maize and was called Chibuku. Or there was always the local Kuche Kuche beer. I decided to just head back to the camp. I was exhausted so upgraded to a dorm room after seeing another ant infestation in my tent. All I wanted was a nice hotel room with air-conditioning and no bugs.

NO BUGS!

***

I woke up the next day refreshed after nine
hours of sleep. Despite my mosquito net above my
bunk bed having holes in it, I didn't get bitten and was
so happy that my sleep had not been disturbed by
anything from the insect species. We would be having
a late start on our way to Mozambique. Because of
the power surge the day before, the computers had
crashed at the Mozambique Embassy in Lilongwe so
they had a backlog of visa applications to process. So
we were departing Mabuya camp at 1 P.M. That
would give me about four hours to clean out the entire
tent of a million ant carcasses.

Once we were on the road, I enjoyed myself by reading magazines until it got dark. It was slow going and we got to the border just in the nick of time before it closed. The guys at the Mozambique immigration office looked like they were having the time of their lives, just joking around with each other. The only two who seemed to be working were the ones stamping passports and even they got sidetracked by the jokesters in the background. The thing to remember if traveling through Mozambique was to have patience. Getting impatient was simply counterproductive.

We entered Mozambique at dusk, along the famous Tete Corridor which used to be known as the "Gun Run". When Mozambique was having a civil war between two political factions and nearly 1 million people died in the conflict, Zimbabwe and Malawi were still trying to trade necessary items between the countries. One convoy a day would be sent to Malawi or Zimbabwe and it would drive at top speed through the war zone in order to deliver necessary goods. Talk about a risky job. The countryside of Mozambique had also been littered with land mines but after the war was over, the Mozambique Government and Western governments worked to get the land cleared of the land mines.

So when told we were going to be bush camping in Mozambique, our natural concern was the land mines, to which our tour leader jokingly said there were no guarantees. Which meant it wasn't a joke. We turned off the lights inside of the truck to attract less attention as it began to get dark. Our driver drove down a dirt road until he found a spot between two fields. We then set up our tents in a semi-circle for security reasons (safety in numbers) around the truck. We built a fire and in the dim light, I could still see figures walking along the road at night, perhaps locals on their way home from work. Now this was real camping, out in the African bush. Being potentially surrounded by land mines just gave it that much more of an edge.

After dinner, we sat around the fire to warm up and then one by one, everyone snuck off to bed early. I mean, what else was there to do? It wasn't like we could go wandering the fields at night.

Chapter Twenty-Two

"The Gun Run"

I was intrigued with Mozambique, even at 5 A.M. the next morning. I had slept deeply and peacefully. I got out of the tent and stretched. It was misty and chilly. A woman farming the next field was already at work, hacking the dark dirt with a hoe. Most Mozambicans work tending small plots with cassava and other crops, and these *machambas* (farm plots) were everywhere.

As we packed up our tents and shoveled down a quick breakfast, the woman gave us a friendly wave. Perhaps another reason I was so intrigued with the country was because I wasn't going to be able to see much of it and the explorer in me was crying out to see more. I gazed out the window as we started our long drive towards Zimbabwe along the Tete

Corridor. The earth looked scorched in some places and the dirt was so dark it was black. Thin trees dotted this sunburnt landscape, heavy with birds' nests. People waved at random from the side of the roads, not quite as frequently as the friendly people of Malawi. I noticed that the women grew their hair out more in Mozambique, in short Afros or cornrowed braids. It was the first time I had seen anyone with an afro in Africa.

The sky was heavy with puffy white clouds and as I looked around, I noticed that all the signs were in Portuguese. Mozambique had been a colony of Portugal and their official language was Portuguese. As we stopped at an intersection in a mid-sized city, I gave a guy a high five after he yelled out "Welcome to Mozambique". I also gave lots of people who waved at me alongside the road the peace sign, which was reciprocated back to me. We reached a full stop in the truck when we came across a traffic accident where someone had died. No matter how long we had to wait, we would still be better off than that poor person. We were going to be extremely late getting into Harare, the capital of Zimbabwe with a population of 2 million and our final destination for the day.

We arrived at the Zimbabwean border around noon. My Zimbabwe visa was $30 and it was the last time I would have to pay for a visa for the rest of the trip because Botswana, Namibia, and South Africa were free for me as an American to enter. The visa processing didn't take so long and we were soon across the border and into Zimbabwe where we made a quick stop at a roadside shop to get refreshments. A woman with sad eyes begged me to buy a can of Coke from her for a dollar. The official currency of Zimbabwe was the US Dollar because the

Zimbabwean currency had crashed. It was a famous currency with 30 billion dollar notes, etc.

In fact, at one point in Zimbabwe, it had cost more to print the note than what it was actually worth. A loaf of bread would cost 30 trillion dollar notes. So, therefore, the currency crashed and it's not hard to see why. Everything was now in US Dollars, making food and other items seem more expensive to me because they were in a currency I knew well. Also, there was no change in Zimbabwe, as in small coins, so even if something was listed as costing $1.75, you would have to pay $2.00 for it because there was no coin change. Sometimes if they had it, the change would be in South African Rand or Botswana Pula. But most likely you would have to buy something to make up the price difference. Also, there was a big problem even getting change in dollars. For example, if you bought something for 5 dollars and you gave a

20 dollar note, the vendors would have a really hard time giving you correct change. No one wanted to take big notes so I was surprised that they even used them.

Once in Zim (as the locals liked to call it), I noticed that the landscape had become almost lunar-like with big piles of boulders and dome-shaped huts that seemed pretty well made with smooth, brick walls and pointed thatched roofs. Zimbabweans, I had heard, liked to have a bush in between them so the huts were a bit more scattered and not so closely huddled together. I imagined in my head that that valley could be called "Valley of the Boulders". In Zimbabwe, about 65% of the population lived in rural areas, while around 40% of the population was under 18 years old. Some of the males had to leave the rural areas to go find work, leaving children and women behind. The average life expectancy was about 40 years.

Kids waved from the side of the road. Waving was an instant mood enhancer because of the smiling kids and people. Strange rock outcrops seemed to spring up from the flat landscape randomly, like large warts. The Msasa tree was the mascot for Zimbabwe and these were dotted about sporadically. I noticed more houses here as opposed to only huts and people seemed a bit more financially well off. I watched a family pumping water out of a well, a man herding his six cattle across the road with a stick, people tending small plots of land, and a woman in full Sunday church wear weeding her garden. I saw a whole field of people wearing white. It was apparently a specific religious group celebrating the 12 apostles. We passed two men, eating *sadza*, white maize meal that looked like mashed potato.

Apparently, the locals loved it and it was often eaten with tomato-based relishes, meat, or gravy.

It started to get dark as we came into the capital city of Harare but I saw lots of nice houses surrounded by barbed wire fences and stone walls studded with shards of glass to prevent people from climbing over. I also saw that all the windows on these houses were barred. The actual houses would not be out of place on any average American street minus all the security. And they were certainly well-protected. I saw people tending gardens and maids sweeping porches. I wondered who lived in those houses and what they did.

It wasn't long before we arrived at camp. After setting up our tents on the great expanse of grass next to a lake and dotted with lovely jacaranda trees, we headed to the camp restaurant where dinner awaited. As we ate, we listened to a white Zimbabwean man talk about the camp's bird sanctuary and all the species of birds they had there. The man was clearly passionate about the birds and the following day, he was giving a walk through the sanctuary and also going to give a bird show, where he would show some of the birds flying around.

I was planning to go into the city the following morning because I heard there was a really good market there. Who could resist that?

Chapter Twenty-Three

"The Capital"

The next morning I was up bright and early to catch a ride on the truck into town with some of the others. We arrived in Harare shortly. It was the first African city which resembled what my definition of a city was, and that was with some tall buildings and a city center. Of course, not everyone's definition is the same but from my point of view, Harare was a real city.

At the Avondale Shops where we were dropped off, there was a huge market selling woodcrafts, woven bags, bowls, clothes, make-up, shoes, sunglasses, etc. It was the best market I had been to so far in Africa simply because besides handcrafts, they sold clothes and other goods. So the selection was better. And the prices were really great.

The vendors were quite aggressive, especially one big-boned lady. She grabbed my arm and wouldn't let me go until I had bought two carved wooden bowls from her for five dollars, which she insisted would shine if you rubbed them with margarine. Later on this feisty woman caught me again, and demanded I buy another bowl from her for two dollars which I couldn't resist. She also demanded that I give her one of my bottles of water. I gave her one of them simply because I was shocked by her confidence and assertiveness bordering on aggressiveness.

A lot of the vendors wanted to chat with me, asking where I was from and if I liked Africa so far. One particularly chatty guy by the name of Thomas wanted to sell me some sunglasses and told me about how he left his small village in the north of Zimbabwe to move to Harare to set up his business of selling sunglasses. Because of the economy and because of Robert Mugabe, the less than sane president of Zimbabwe, not as many people were visiting Zimbabwe so everyone suffered and no one was making money, he explained. He was trying to make enough money to pay for his brother's school fees. It was hard for me to hear sad story after sad story. I bought a pair of sunglasses from Thomas and then asked him what he liked to do in his free time. Listening to Bob Marley and hanging out with his friends were at the top of his list.

Everyone wanted to leave early whereas I could have easily spent the whole afternoon wandering aimlessly in the market. But I did end up with three bowls and the sunglasses. Oh, and some of the old Zimbabwean currency, that I bought off of a guy selling notes of bills that said, 30 billion, etc. I also noticed that the two-dollar bill was in circulation in Zimbabwe, a very rare note to find back in the U.S.

Before leaving the city, I ran into the supermarket to grab some tissues which were listed as being $1.25. I gave $2.00. They had no change and gave me the choice of either buying something for 75 cents to make up for it, or having the supermarket write me up a voucher for the next time I shopped. I opted for a small bottle of water for fifty cents. What a pain it would be to shop like this every day of your life. Also, none of the vendors at the market would give change. If you wanted a two dollar item and gave them ten dollars, they would add in a couple of things and tell you that you could get it all for ten dollars. Perhaps that was their way of trying to make a bigger sale.

We all piled into a taxi van to get back to the camp, fitting eleven people into a seven-seater van. It cost us four dollars each to get back which wasn't too terrible because it was about a thirty-minute drive to the campsite. The taxi driver said that he wasn't too busy these days because everyone was in a bad mood as they were waiting on the rains to come. The rains were late and it wasn't good for the farmers or for anyone. He was surprised to hear that there were droughts in both North America and Europe in the most recent summer months and I was guessing that he didn't check the international news much.

Back at the camp, I decided to find the two zebras that had been wandering around. Yes, there were two wild zebras grazing on the campsite grounds, followed by a lone sheep who *thought* he was a zebra. I eventually found the zebras munching away on the grass, along with their friend, the sheep, behind some outhouses. They barely noticed my presence and I crept toward them slowly. I was probably two yards away. I sat and watched them for a while until one of them started to walk towards me briskly without stopping. So I decided to hide behind a tree as a shield. It worked and he soon forgot about me and went back to grazing.

It was also time for the bird walk. The camp had a variety of birds which they had rescued and were breeding. The man who led the walk, named John, showed us an eagle that blushed when excited (its face went from yellow to pink and back again), two huge vultures, and an array of exotic birds. It was interesting to hear about each of the birds. I learned that there are lots of people in Africa who believe vultures can predict death, and the birds are therefore killed if caught. Another morbid superstition they have is that if an owl lands on your roof, someone in that house will die soon. The Zimbabweans spoke in a clipped accent that was similar to the South African accent and said things like, "howz it?" when they greeted each other.

Gary, the owner of the camp, had had a hard time in Zimbabwe with the government. When the government passed various land reformation acts in the 90s and early 2000s, they tried to take all the white farmers' land to give to the Zimbabwe war vets who came back from war. It was their idea of a land "redistribution" scheme. However, not only did a lot of white people of European descent who had lived in Zimbabwe all of their lives lose their land, many black farm workers lost their jobs in the process and no land was redistributed to them. Gary had lost one of his farms and was also still fighting the government for his land. Despite his hardships, he was a very jolly fellow who seemed to always be laughing and smiling.

According to an article published in May 2013 in the Guardian newspaper from the UK, Robert Mugabe, the current leader of Zimbabwe, had come

under recent scrutiny for the land reformation act.
"Farm buildings ablaze, war veterans on the rampage
and white farmers emerging bloodied and bruised are
among the defining images of the case against the
Zimbabwean president, Robert Mugabe", the article
had quoted.

In 2000, war veterans had launched a quick
scheme land-distribution program. This was launched
as an attempt to "correct the colonialist legacy that
left vast tracts of land in the hands of a complacent
white minority."

What had happened is that white farmers who
had been successful at farming had had their land
taken by war veterans that didn't have any farming
skills. Most of the land went into disarray. The
government had promised the "new" farmers
equipment for farming and that promise had fallen
through, leaving vast tracts of land unused. According

to Paul Theroux's Dark Star Safari, Mugabe had actively encouraged veterans of the guerilla war who were classed as "landless peasants" to invade, occupy, and squat in the fields of white farmers and take their land by force. Ten percent of white farmers had been murdered by these invaders. None of the murderers had been prosecuted and instead were congratulated for seizing the land.

According to the article in The Guardian, "Food production nosedived and one of Africa's strongest economies shrank to half the size it had been in 1980."

Today there are many critics over Mugabe's and Zanu-PF policies. Some say the land reformation made it possible for many smaller and poorer farmers to now become successful (and who would have never had the chance to do so) while others say that the farmers who are out of work and lost their jobs under the land reformation scheme outnumber the new farmers. Land is a tricky thing and redistribution of it has never been easy, as shown in Zimbabwe and also in Israel/Palestine. Although these were completely different situations, as we have seen in history, land redistribution always has problems.

We watched the bird show next, and Gary explained that two of his birds (one of which was the African fish eagle) had been used on David Attenborough's "Life of Birds" BBC documentary which was pretty impressive. He explained that a lot of the shots were set up and not necessarily in the wild but I guess there was no way to find all the birds in the wild and track them as it would take ages. Although it made sense, I didn't want to tell him that he had just taken all the magic out of BBC documentaries with David Attenborough. But that didn't mean I would ever stop watching them.

Chapter Twenty-Four

"Chimanimani"

Zimbabwe was rich with diamonds. Well, that is what a white Zimbabwean man had told one of us on the way to Chimanimani National Park. According to him, in the not so recent past, buckets of diamonds used to be sold on the streets for about 300 dollars a bucket. I couldn't believe it. Zimbabwe was set to become the world's next top producer of diamonds after Botswana. A lot of Russians were trying to get involved in the diamond business in Zimbabwe. They had supplied Zimbabwe with guns and ammo during their war so according to this man, now it was time to get their back scratched by the Zimbabweans. The Chinese were also working in the diamond mines, hired by the Zimbabwean government because they were fast, efficient workers who worked for a very low wage.

We arrived in the late afternoon to the tiny town of Chimanimani, which was settled in the valley at the foot of a beautiful range of green and rocky mountains that had jagged outlines against the bright blue sky. The town was no more than one restaurant, a tiny market, and two small shops. The campsite was beautiful and the landscape reminded me of an elegant country estate with manicured gardens and a swimming pool.

While I was setting up my tent I shuddered when I saw huge ants crawling about, the biggest ants I had ever seen. One of them was carrying a baby millipede for its dinner. I just hoped they would keep to themselves and stay out of my tent. There was an option to do a hike the following day in the Chimanimani National Park. I really wanted to do it but was also feeling a little under the weather. What I needed was a good day of rest in the sun. The swimming pool beckoned.

***

The next day was a free day and the first one in which I would finally be able to get some sleep. Unfortunately, someone in the village had decided to honk their truck horn starting from 4 A.M. in the morning until about 9 A.M. So my plan to sleep in didn't really work. So I grumpily got up, had breakfast, and decided to lay by the pool and work on my tan. The rest of the day passed leisurely.

I decided to walk into the village after lunch. The locals were seemingly friendly. I stopped in a little food mart where dusty cans of tomatoes and other food items lined the shelves. They all looked to be about ten years old and way past their expiry date.

There wasn't much choice and as I was browsing, one of the teenaged female staff in the shop asked me where I was from and what I was doing in Africa.

"What are your plans for Christmas?" she enquired, as though she might ask me around for her family gathering.

"I'm going to Namibia for Christmas this year, to Spitzkoppe," I replied.

"I want to go with you. Please take me with you," she said. "I am bored here."

She walked up to me and began to touch my hair, as though I was a living exhibit. She giggled.

"You are pretty," she said, giggling some more.

I said thank you and quickly purchased a dusty packet of ginger cookies for the road. It was time to explore what else was in the village.

From the food mart, there wasn't much to see except for a tiny market where an elderly woman approached me.

"You buy?" she asked me, pointing to a pair of women's underwear that she was selling.

"No thank you. I already some," I said to her.

"Please give me some of them," she said, suddenly serious.

I laughed.

"I'm sorry but I don't have any extra to give you at the moment.

A look of disappointment flashed across her face. What was it with this village?

A few small kids followed me and screamed out "how are you?!" and "I'm fine!" when inquired about their well-being. They wanted me to give them high-fives, which of course I did. I bought a maize-meal energy drink that I had been noticing and wanted to try. It was 50 cents so I had to buy something else to make it one dollar since no one had change for 50 cents. Outside of the store, I took a sip. It was horrible. I had bought a banana-flavored one to try and disguise the taste a little bit but it didn't help. It tasted like liquid ugali (maize meal paste) and although I didn't mind ugali, I don't think it should have ever been made into a liquid form.

Back at the camp, I went to the bar to get inside as it was nearing dusk. It was so chilly at the foot of those mountains. On one hand it was a relief from the heat but on the other well, it was just uncomfortable. That night there was a bachelorette party being held there for a local woman. Loud African music was pounding the walls and the women seemed to be having a ball as they laughed up a storm and danced around. The tradition was for the bride to ask for a certain amount of money from the guests but hide behind a blanket while doing this. Once all the money had been collected, she would come out from behind the blanket and rejoin the party. I guess it saved the embarrassment of having to tell your guests what kind of gifts you wanted. Problem solved.

Chapter Twenty-Five

"The Great Zimbabwe Ruins"

The next morning, trouble with the truck's battery made us late getting on the road. We were heading to the Great Zimbabwe Ruins, the largest ruins in sub-Saharan Africa, a settlement that had existed from the 11th century to the 17th century and had once thrived. It was a chance to peek at what was going on in Zimbabwe nearly a thousand years ago.

We arrived at the camp next to the ruins around 3 P.M. and immediately left to do the walk. Our guide's name was Courage, which wasn't unusual in Africa where people named their children things like Blessings, Hope, and Harmony. He was at student a local college and was studying archaeology. He hadn't been outside of Zimbabwe but had traveled to a few other sites of archaeological interest outside of the Great Zimbabwe Ruins.

Courage led us through the site, explaining along the way. The Great Zimbabwe Ruins were the remains of a very old city that had first been occupied in the 11th century. The city had grown wealthy, due to the Swahili gold trade and it wasn't long before it became a powerful religious and political capital. However, as history has shown before, all great things do eventually come to an end. By the 15th century, the people of Great Zimbabwe had depleted the natural resources of the land and had to leave. When the Portuguese arrived in the 16th century, the city was deserted.

The site was divided into several major ruins of which there was the Hill Complex, the Valley, and the Great Enclosure, which is thought to have served as a royal compound. We also walked through the

Parallel Passage. It may have been a means of moving from the northern entrance to a large conical tower without being detected by those within the enclosure.

While I was inside the museum at the site, I was looking at some items that were traded at the Great Zimbabwe Ruins with other countries such as Persia and China.

"Those bowls over there that were traded then are still being sold today in China," I said to courage, pointing to a set of bowls in a very popular Chinese pattern.

"Are you Chinese? Which city are you from?" he asked me, suddenly interested.

I paused for a moment, wondering if he was serious. I have blonde hair, green eyes, and very pale skin, the very opposite of a person of Chinese descent (besides perhaps the pale skin).

"Actually I'm not Chinese, I'm from America," I replied and he looked slightly confused. It turned out he was serious. Another African guy had asked another Caucasian girl on our trip previously if she was from Taiwan. I really don't think the Africans that we had encountered could tell the difference between Asian and Caucasian people because to them, we both had white skin. Perhaps we all looked the same to them.

***

The next day we were off to Antelope Park, situated near Gweru, Zimbabwe. Along the way, we stopped at a stone market, where of course I ended up buying an entire Noah's Ark worth of stone-carved animals that I wasn't intending to buy. And it was fun to buy them. The reason was because the vendors accepted clothes for trade. I really enjoyed this part about some African markets. I could exchange some clothes that I didn't really need any more for some souvenirs. So at this market, I traded a pair of pajama pants and a sparkly top for a small table cover plus five dollars. I also bought two stone carvings, two of them for 7 dollars and also miniature bookends and stone carvings of animals.

"Please sister, please buy some more. I need to pay for my sister's school fees," the woman whose crafts I was looking through pleaded.

Her deals kept getting better and better, and finally I had to just walk away because I was out of money. This is the kind of thing that happened to me often at African markets, or any market in general. The ladies *especially* were good at making sales.

We arrived in Antelope Park in the afternoon, in time to hear a video presentation and learn about some of the work they did with lions. Antelope Park is a game park situated in 3000 acres of savannah and is home to the famous ALERT Program in regards to lion rehabilitation. Their intention was to rehabilitate captive bred lions into a limited number of semi-wild environments (stage three), free of any human contact. According to the program, "the self-sustaining and socially stable wild-living prides will give birth to cubs that will be raised by the pride in their natural environment; such that they have natural skills comparable to any wild-borne lion. As such they can be reintroduced into appropriate national parks and reserves, identified for their protection."

They were raising lions to eventually release them back into the wild as the lion population had decreased by 80-90 percent all over Africa. There were four stages of the process, with Stage Four being their release back into the wild.

I decided to do the cub viewing and the lion walk. The cub viewing was simply that, a chance to pet and see the baby lion cubs. The lion walk allowed people to walk in the African bush with two lions that were two-years-old. At two-years-old they were very big though, and it was exciting to see that this opportunity was offered. When I say big, I mean big enough to probably eat you. But what is life without risk?

It looked like my chance to get up close and personal with lions had finally arrived.

Chapter Twenty-Six

"Antelope Park Should Be Called Lion Park"

The next day I woke up in anticipation of the cub viewing and lion walk. After a hot shower and nice breakfast, I headed to the first activity, the cub viewing. A small group of us were ushered into a large grassy enclosure where two adorable baby cubs with big sweet eyes and large clumsy-looking paws waited on a bed of straw. They had faces to instantly love. They were siblings, one male and one female. They followed the guide, who held out a buffalo horn for them to play with.

It seemed that we had caught them at their laziest. They weren't really interested in playing and instead were more interested in being docile and lazy, enjoying belly rubs and pats on the head. Because they were feeling rather lazy, it was easy to get pictures with them. They were adorable, with their big doe-like brown eyes, large faces, and oversized paws. The male one started to lick my arm, which was simply charming. It was a peaceful gesture. The lion cubs communicated by head rubbing and nuzzling each other. It was a kind of greeting but was also common after an animal had been apart from others, or after a fight. They were only four months old. We stayed in the enclosure with them for about thirty minutes and I was sad to leave them in the end.

After the cub viewing, it was time for my lion walk. These lions were in Stage One, which meant that they were still learning to hunt and getting used to the African bush. So the lion walks were actually allowing them to walk around the bush and look for prey. We were able to walk beside them while they did this, which was really amazing and also somewhat dangerous (although we were assured that it was not).

There was a safety presentation before the walk, where the guides told us not to wear anything with a red color, no dangly bits hanging off of your clothes, and no crouching on the ground because the lions identified largeness with eye-level and height. So if you were double the height of the lion, it actually thought that you were twice the size. We were also meant to stay in a group because the lions saw us as a pride, or a group of animals. Any "animal" that wandered off would be seen as weak and fragile and the lion may stalk it. So there was not to be any wandering off. We weren't to run, leave anything on the ground, or disobey any other rule. It was all sounding quite serious and it made me feel a little bit nervous to go.

We hopped in the back of a Jeep and were soon off into the bush and the grasslands of the savannah. We arrived minutes later to see two large golden-haired lions lying on the ground, waiting for us. It was intimidating to see these two beautiful beasts since we would be walking beside them. We hopped out of the Jeep and were soon on the ground next to the lions. Like the guides, we carried long sticks, just in case you wanted to use the stick as a kind of arm extension. In that case, the lion would bite the stick rather than your actual arm.

We began to walk with the lions (I would say their heads reached just above my waist) and it was great to just be there with them. The handlers were really good; they told us when to stay together and told us to walk closely to the lion when we were able to do so. They also took our cameras off of our hands and took lots and lots of great shots. We walked along until we came to a small dirt mound. The lions climbed on top of it and I stood behind them as the handlers stood around and took pictures. They were really good with the lions and the lions obeyed them. We continued walking and occasionally the lions would stop and let us pat their backs. Their fur felt coarse to the touch and when I looked at my hand, it was covered in lion hair. They shed just as badly as domesticated cats. Sometimes, the lions would just flop to the ground and didn't want to get back up to walk again. We continued walking with them and then watched them run off into the savannah. The guide said that they had stalked and killed a wildebeest before and they were still learning to hunt. The previous day they had stalked a zebra but the zebra kicked them so they weren't able to catch it.

Lions tended to stalk their prey in groups but they weren't known for their stamina. They could only run fast in short bursts and needed to be close their prey before attacking. Many killed prey at night, under the cover of darkness. The lionesses were the hunters of a pride, and they were also more aggressive than the males. Lionesses worked together to hunt and often circled the prey from different points. Lions killed prey by strangling them but smaller prey could sometimes be killed by just a swipe from the lion's paw. When it was all over, I still couldn't believe I had walked with an adolescent lion that could have knocked me out with one swipe. Where else in the world could you do that?

Chapter Twenty-Seven

"On the Way to the 7ᵗʰ Wonder"

After leaving Antelope Park, we spent two nights in Bulawayo and Matobo National Park and then left for Victoria Falls, one of the Seven Wonders of the World. Vic Falls straddled the border between Zambia and Zimbabwe. The locals called Victoria Falls by another name, Mosi-oa-Tunya, which meant "the smoke that thunders", a name I considered more appropriate. The reason I thought that was because even from a distance, you could see the mist rising from the oozing wetland and hear the deep roar of the torrent.

We arrived in the late afternoon. The weather was steamy and hot. The small town of Victoria Falls was located within the national park and the only danger listed in Lonely Planet was that at dawn and dusk, there was danger of lions, elephants, etc. roaming the streets. It was reason enough to be nervous. However, our tour leader said that according to the locals, there was no danger from lions, only elephants. And of course, the usual suspects of warthogs and baboons.

David Livingstone, the Scottish missionary and explorer, is believed to have been the first European to set eyes upon Victoria Falls on November 17th, 1855. Livingstone named his discovery in honor of Queen Victoria, but the indigenous name, Mosi-oa-Tunya is also well known. He wrote of the falls, *"No one can imagine the beauty of the view from anything witnessed in England. It had never been seen before by European eyes; but scenes so lovely must have been gazed upon by angels in their flight."*

When we arrived at the camp, we immediately put our tents up and then headed to Shoestrings café and bar to hear a talk about what we could do in Vic Falls. Of the activities offered, you could bungee jump, go river rafting, and go to Devil's Pool, which was literally a pool on the edge of the waterfalls on the Zambian side. When the river flow was at a certain level, usually between September and December, a rock barrier formed a whirlpool with minimal current, allowing swimmers to splash around in relative safety a few feet from the point where the water plunged over the side into oblivion. Because I had never heard of Devil's Pool before coming to Vic Falls I hadn't applied for a double-entry visa to Zimbabwe when I had entered the country. So that meant that unfortunately I couldn't go as I didn't have permission to cross into Zambia.

After Shoestrings, a few of us went to the local supermarket to pick up some wine as we were planning to go out that night. Purchasing a bottle of Shiraz had become a real treat as I hadn't been able to purchase wine in East Africa due to the high price. However, wine was cheaper in Southern Africa and I could finally afford to buy some.

Victoria Falls, the town, was centered on tourism and was very safe to walk around. The only annoying thing was that there were lots of local men walking around trying to sell the old Zimbabwean currency, small carvings of animals, etc. who were absolutely relentless at trying to make a sale. The sellers were not actually allowed to sell on the street to tourists and the good thing was that when the police walked by, they scattered like the wind.

Back at the camp, a few us made dinner and had some drinks. I couldn't even sit down to enjoy my wine, I had to stand up and move every so often because of the mosquitoes. The mosquitoes in Vic Falls were vicious, blood-sucking little devils! They were intent on feasting on me. There were also Vervet monkeys everywhere, watching to see if we left behind any food that they could take. They were so naughty, those monkeys, and I could see their eyes shining in the darkness from the tree branches above.

After dinner, we met the others at the Shoestrings bar where there was great music playing. Where there was music, I would always follow. We danced for a while and then walked to a casino further down the street. The casino was surprisingly nice, a tiny slice of Las Vegas in Southern Africa which was strangely out of place needless to say. Inside there was a dance club and at the club they were having a Miss Wild Thing contest. Despite the name, the contest was very tame. Africa is quite conservative and Miss Wild Thing was actually a fashion show/pageant. The contestants wore 80s-style prom dresses and strutted down a makeshift runway at the front of the club. A local rapper rapped during an intermission, wearing a huge golden chain of a dollar sign.

On the way back to the camp later, I spotted two huge African elephants walking toward me down the street, their ears flapping and their tusks almost glowing in the dark. I quickly moved out of their way and incredulously watched them walk off into a group of trees. I had to pinch myself to believe it was real.

Chapter Twenty-Eight

"Wonders of the World"

Today was the day I was going to see Victoria Falls from the Zimbabwean side. It was 30 dollars to enter the park and it was within walking distance from the camp. Even from the camp, I could hear the pulsing current of the Zambezi River and had been falling asleep to the surprisingly relaxing sound every night.

On the way there, I was followed by about four vendors who tried to sell me a variety of things such as elephant hair bracelets, snake figurine necklaces, and lion tooth charms.

"Hey, sister!" they called out.

They seemed to be in charge of separate territories, which was quite good as it was fair for everyone and gave them all a good chance to target all the tourists walking by. Good for them and bad for the tourists. When they reached the end of their territory, a new person would start following me. It was like a vendor relay race and whoever managed to sell something to a tourist won. Somehow, without me promising anything, they had managed to put the words into my mouth that I would buy something from them once I left the Falls and walked back up the street. They were confident that after a few hours, I would have completely changed my mind and would go on a wild shopping spree up the streets of Victoria Falls.

Once inside the Falls, I made my way around to each viewing point. The Falls were beautiful and the main part gushed with so much force onto the rocks below, it was hypnotic to watch. I sat for a while, listening to the hollow sound of the Falls. I calculated that on the main part of the Falls, it took three seconds for the water to reach the bottom from the top of the waterfall.

Near the next viewing point, there was a statue of David Livingstone. The statue stated that his heart was buried in Zambia and his further remains were buried in Westminster Abbey in England in the Explorers Corner. But his heart would remain in Africa forever, that was for sure.

The viewpoints kept getting better and better and there was mist everywhere, rippling and rolling in the sunlight. It wasn't long before I was soaked. I watched as the swollen Zambezi tumbled off the side of the sheer cliffs. There were shimmering rainbows everywhere at the foot of the various falls, as the mist rose slowly up from the gushing water. At one point, I could see straight across to Devil's Pool on the Zambian side. People were literally on the edge of a huge drop off. The guides took the people by boat to a specific point on the river and then they had to jump

off of a rock into the Devil's Pool, which was right on

the top of the main part of Victoria Falls.

Unfortunately, one guide had slipped and fallen the

year before which was tragic as there was no way you

could survive if that happened. At first, when I saw

the guide jump in, I thought someone was committing

suicide, that's how close it was to the edge. But then

of course, I couldn't see the rock wall underneath the

water. It looked pretty incredible.

I continued all the way to the end of the

walkway, to Rainbow Falls (where there is always a

rainbow at the foot of about five separate waterfalls

pouring from the side of a sheer rock wall) and to a

huge gorge filled with churning green water. This was

where the rafting began on the Zambezi River.

Apparently, it was rumored that the location was the

best white water rafting was in the whole world, with

intense currents around every bend in the rock-studded water. I continued on to a long bridge, where I coincidentally happened to see one of my tour leaders bungee jump off the bridge. The views were incredibly scenic and it was amazing to see this wonder of the world.

After seeing the Falls, I made my way out and headed to the local market. Perhaps the vendors had put some sort of subliminal message in my brain. Maybe I was going to buy something after all! What I really wanted was a woven straw handbag with a leather strap and clasp that came in colors of black, reddish brown, and white. I had been looking for the bag since a market in Harare. Fortunately, I found one guy named Patience at the market in Vic Falls who had the bag but he only had one of them. In my own handbag, I found a few items to trade if necessary, including sweets from America, socks, and mosquito repellent. I tried to lure him with these to get a discount.

"What else do you have?" he asked me, grinning a mischievous smile. "What is this?" he asked, pointing to a flash of metal at the bottom of my bag.

"That's my thermos. I'm not trading it," I replied.

"Just let me see it," he said, not taking his eyes off my bag.

I showed him the thermos but insisted I wasn't trading it. I tried to put on a strong front and offered twelve dollars for the bag plus the stuff I had offered to trade. Stubborn as a mule, he shook his head and pointed to the thermos.

"I will be back tomorrow," I told him.

Sometimes you had to play hard to get. So we agreed that we would both think about it and I would come back the following day. Perhaps I had to up my game.

***

The next day was my last day in Victoria Falls. I went to the market to see Patience, where I finally managed to get the bag I had wanted. In the end, I had to throw in a dress, more sweets, a face towel, and a nice shirt to complete the deal. But I kept the thermos. As I continued to shop, I got harassed (the most appropriate word to describe it) by several more vendors who looked better dressed than me but who said they had no money for food, etc. I hated to doubt their story. It might have been true, that they were particularly poor but somehow, with this particular group, I had my reservations. This particular market was really stressful and I wasn't surprised to hear that someone in our group had actually started to cry because they got hassled so much. Everyone wanted a piece of me. Some of the vendors said that they had seen me around the last few days and seriously, they *really* did know who I was. They all knew that I was looking for a bag and here, word traveled fast.

One guy named King George said that he was upset that I hadn't visited his shop from the previous day and basically led me by the arm there. Although I had a look around, I finally had to say that I didn't want to buy anything. Instead, I offered him some candy as a peace offering which I was relieved that he accepted with a smile. Perhaps that was the secret at markets, to come loaded with candy to give out to vendors with whom you bought nothing from.

That night we had a going away party for some of the people from our trip who were leaving

and went back to Shoestrings. One local guy talking
to the group of us, introduced himself.

"My job is as a poacher, I poach elephants for
ivory!" he exclaimed, laughing. "I can get 500,000
British pounds for every tusk and I only have to do
one every five years to survive."

The way he said it was so nonchalant that I
and everyone else thought he was serious. A few of us
got up to leave the table, saying we didn't agree with
his profession.

"Haha, I am not a poacher, I am a rafting
guide. I like to play this joke on tourists," he said,
bursting out with laughter.

His brother, who was with him, was into
weight lifting and he was ripped. In all seriousness,
when he found out I was from America, he asked me
to bring him Muscle Milk protein powder the next
time I was in town. Now it was my turn to laugh.

Chapter Twenty-Nine

"Welcome to Botswana!"

I had always been intrigued with Botswana ever since I read a few books from the popular series of the *Number One Ladies Detective Agency* by Alexander McCall Smith. The series was about a detective agency in Botswana, run by two ladies who spend their time doing paperwork, solving small mysteries, and drinking red bush tea. From reading the books, I gathered that the people of Botswana have a very proud belief in both their government and country. As in other African countries, respect for elders, religious beliefs, and traditional gender roles are at the heart of culture in Botswana. There is also the practice of using the *kgotla*, which is a specially designated meeting place in each village where grievances can be aired in an atmosphere of mutual respect.

Upon arrival in Botswana, we had to wipe our feet on a chemical-soaked mat and dump all of our fruits and veggies in the trash. Dumping the fruit was done to prevent fruit flies from spreading. The wiping of feet was to prevent foot and mouth disease. At immigration, there was even a machine dispensing free condoms for AIDS prevention which was a hopeful sign. Things were looking more organized in Botswana. However, even after entering, there were still two more road checks further on to see if we had brought in any fruits or veggies or perhaps had forgotten to wipe our feet on the chemical mat.

Botswana was better off than the countries north of it, perhaps because it is the world's largest exporter of diamonds. What struck me about the landscape of Botswana was that the land was very flat; there were no mountains or hills all the way from Vic Falls to Maun, the gateway to the Okavango Delta. The soil was a sandy one and clusters of trees grew out of it sporadically. Another vast difference was that I hardly saw anyone on the roads, or even living near the roads.

The country looked deserted compared to the busy roads of Kenya, Uganda, and Malawi. I barely saw any African huts but did see the occasional cow along the side of the road. Someone said they spotted a giraffe and a few elephants earlier in the day but I hadn't seen them. In fact, I hardly saw a human or animal soul in sight.

Botswana, like the rest of Africa, has had its share of colonial history from the Boer War of the later 1800s to the interesting coupling of a Tswana chief, Seretse Khama and Ruth Williams of England (Lady Khama). The current president of Botswana,

Ian Khama is the son of these two. The story of how Seretse and Ruth met went like this. In 1923, Chief Khama III died and was succeeded by his son Sekgoma, who died only two years later. The heir to the throne, four-year-old Seretse Khama, wasn't ready for the job, so his 21-year-old uncle, Tshekedi Khama became the head of the clan.

After WWII, Seretse Khama went to study in England where he met and married Ruth. Tshekedi Khama was furious at this breach of tribal custom, and apartheid-era South African authorities were none too happy either. The British government blocked Seretse's chieftaincy and he was exiled to England. Bitterness continued until 1956 when Seretse Khama renounced his right to power and returned with his wife to Botswana to serve as a minor official.

When Botswana became independent in 1966, the black and white stripes on the new flag were primarily influenced by the zebra and the stripes were meant to represent the harmony between people of different races and ethnicities in Botswana. This was why I liked Botswana. I think that they had made a clear statement with their flag for racial harmony between blacks and whites. Botswana had seen the apartheid era events in South Africa and had moved one step forward. The fact that zebras are almost completely harmless and peaceful animals makes me love the flag of Botswana ever more. Two zebras also adorn the Botswana coat of arms, which shows that the animal is a symbol of national unity.

In fact, Botswana's love of zebras has even been shown in an old Tswana folktale that tells the story of how the animal got its fashionable marks. According to the legend, one day the Creator of the earth called all animals that wore drab coats to have their hides decorated. As there were many animals in the line waiting their turn, the zebra got agitated and kicked the paint container that the Creator was holding and the paint splashed on his back and that led to him having the stripes. I couldn't help but thinking that Botswana had already charmed me.

For our first night in Botswana we were camping on the banks of the Chobe River. The Chobe National Park and riverfront was home to an abundance of wildlife. Almost every southern-African mammal species existed there.

We arrived at the camp after lunch in Kasane and quickly got ready to go on the Chobe River safari cruise. Once we had boarded the boat, we were soon gliding down the steely gray river at a leisurely pace. Within minutes we had spotted freshwater crocodiles and hippos in the water and along the banks. A multitude of birds, including the African fish eagle could be seen in this unique landscape. The river ran like a main artery through lush green flatlands, and multiple veins of it spread through the land. From a distance, I spotted large, grayish-brown animals on a patch of green near the river's edge. At first I thought they were elephants but as we got closer I saw they were hippos! There were about twelve of them, all grazing near the water. Hippos were semi-aquatic and territorial bulls presided over a stretch of river and groups of females with their young. At dusk, they often emerged from the water to graze on the grass. It was amazing to see them outside of the water. I had seen them previously in Kenya in the water but had not seen them on land. I was thrilled to see these amazing animals, whose closest living relatives are whales and porpoises (despite the hippos' resemblance to pigs). In Africa, fossils of hippopotamus prints have been found and have been dated back to 16 million years ago!

Hippos were most comfortable in the water and on land they felt vulnerable. Perhaps that was why as we edged closer to the bank of the river where the hippos were grazing, one by one, they jumped (or rather slid) into the water. In the distance, I saw a baby hippo and the mother running. Hippos could outrun Usain Bolt, the fastest man in the world who won the gold medal for Jamaica in the Olympics for sprinting. I couldn't imagine that these huge beasts could run fast but they actually could! The hippos were everywhere around us, both in and out of the water. Even when you didn't expect to see them, a head would pop up out of the water.

In addition to hippos, I saw a multitude of crocs and various kinds of birds. Further on, we saw a herd of elephants. In the middle of them was a tiny elephant that was clearly being guarded by the bigger ones. It was so cute with its tiny trunk. The elephants came to the water's edge to get a drink. Two African buffaloes lay on the grass by the water's edge as well. The guide said they were old ones that had "retired" from the heard and moved to a quieter place.

African buffaloes are very dangerous animals. With their massive helmet-like horns, I wasn't surprised. If they ran for you, well, you better run for your life. The buffaloes each had about three small white birds called oxpeckers that perched on their backs and picked off insects. One of the birds was even nestled in the groin region of the buffalo lying on the ground. All I can say is that they must have been fairly comfortable with each other.

A number of antelope such as impala and waterboks grazed along the peaceful river and I even spotted the impressive kudu with its long, twisted horns that point skywards. The kudu are huge and have a few white stripes in a kind of wavy pattern.

They are beautifully dangerous but can be taken down by a pack of painted dogs. Like many other antelope, male kudu can be found in bachelor groups, but they are more likely to be solitary. When males do have a face-off, they will lock their horns in a competition to determine the stronger puller. Sometimes two competing males are unable to unlock their horns and, if unable to disengage, will die of starvation or dehydration.

I liked seeing the scenery along the Chobe, it was a peaceful one with all the vegetarian animals grazing peacefully side by side. A South African couple on the boat told me that there were lions further into the national park and they had seen them on the water's edge before. Our tour guide also mentioned to us that a hippo had wandered into the camp the last time they were there and they had found it wandering around the tents and the overland truck. I was really glad that I hadn't been there for that. The hippo had not been looking for trouble but could have crushed anyone with its one ton body weight. The security guards had had to find a way to scare it out of the camp and it had eventually left.

We arrived back at the camp just in time for sunset. The sun dropped into the horizon, filling the sky with a painter's strokes of pink, orange, and purple. Fluffy clouds were outlined in the multitude of colors and changed shades with the setting sun. The river then took on the color of the sky and gentle waves shimmered under the vibrant hues. Two hippos played in the water and nothing could be heard but the occasional splash as the sun set on the Chobe River. It was the perfect ending to the perfect day in Botswana.

Chapter Thirty

"Makoros"

We traveled from the Chobe River to the Sepia Hotel in Maun the following day. It was a really long day, with about ten hours of driving. We stopped in Maun to quickly get some groceries and I browsed a local food shop where I found *megunya*, also known as fat cakes, which are fried pieces of dough, much like a doughnut. I also found a hot food bar where I picked up some maize meal, called *pap* in Botswana. I was hoping to find some ladies selling bags of deep fried mopane worms, a local delicacy but I didn't see anyone. I did see *bojalwa*, an inexpensive, sprouted sorghum beer which was brewed commercially as Chibuku. I had tried it in Zimbabwe and it simply tasted like yeast.

After leaving Maun, we headed to the Sepia Hotel. Our first order of the evening was paying for our two nights and three day trip into the Okavango Delta. I had some old and battered U.S. dollars that I had received in Zimbabwe as change, but they wouldn't accept them in Botswana so I was stuck with them. I wasn't even sure they would be accepted in the U.S.

The Okavango Delta is the world's largest inland delta, a web of water that has flooded the grasslands and which sustains vast quantities of wildlife. We would be going into the Delta for two nights and we would be bush camping. We would be guided there by a local guide who would row us out in traditional *makoro* canoes. And we were leaving the following morning. So we had the evening to pack up our things and take showers since the only shower we would be having for the next two days would be a "Delta shower".

***

The next morning I packed up my sleeping bag along with my tent and daily necessities for the next couple of days and hopped in a four-wheel drive along with the others. We were headed to the point along the Delta where we would get into our *makoros* and meet our guides. The day was warm and dry and the sun was shining brightly in the sky. We passed through Maun and then hit the dirt roads in a cloud of dust.

As we passed through local villages, kids waved to us from the side of the dirt road. I could tell when we were getting closer to the Delta because I started to see lots of overland company tents in local's backyards. In one area, there was a tiny village of tents, probably donated by backpackers or overland companies. It was really interesting to see the locals using the tents so enthusiastically.

We arrived at the banks of the Okavango Delta soon after. The guides were there and waiting to load all of our stuff onto the narrow canoes. My guide's name was Bothle (pronounced as Beth), a very traditional Botswanan name. I somehow managed to fit in all of my stuff into this *makoro* canoe which was barely wider than me. The traditional canoes were made of wood from the mopane tree but since the Botswana government was trying to save trees, most people used canoes made of fiberglass.

The day was peaceful and the water in the Delta sparkled in the sun. The Delta was really no more than a huge flooded plain of water that had veered off into many different waterways lined with reeds. There were hundreds of white water lilies floating on the surface of the dark water, attached to a thick pink cord that reached down into the depths of the water to the earth below. The water for the most part was shallow and it was a dark color that looked like red bush tea from all the minerals in the water that had seeped into it.

Once everyone had gotten into the *makoros*, we were off. The guides had a long wooden pole that they used to push us through the water and reeds. The channels were so narrow sometimes, no wider than the boat itself and reeds were constantly hitting me in the face. To be at that level of the water gave me an interesting perspective of actually *being* in the water. I felt like I was actually a part of the Delta and that I was seeing it firsthand. It was different from being on a regular boat because the sides of the *makoro* were almost submerged in the water, so it felt like I was gliding on top of it. I have heard a similar sensation described by those on motorcycles in that they really feel the environments that they ride through.

It was really peaceful in the canoes as we glided through. The sky stretched for miles ahead and the sun played through spaces in the reeds, casting a dancing light on the water. In some parts of the channels, the water was so still that it had become a mirror reflection for whatever was above it. We glided along the edge of a bigger channel and the sudden splashing of a hippo emerging from the water with gusto surprised everyone. The hippos were dangerous of course so we couldn't travel by canoes in the middle of the channel, otherwise we were intruding on their territory. The hippo gazed at us as we glided by and the only thing visible above the water were its eyes and little ears. The hippos were like submarines, popping up here and there to view their surroundings, but trying to not reveal too much about themselves at the same time. We passed the hippo safely. He was by himself. The guide said that he was most likely kicked out of a group of hippos and was now alone and angry. He would return to the pack at a later time, steal two females, and then start his own family by himself.

We continued on through the reed channels for about forty-five minutes before arriving at the place where we would camp. We were in the middle of the Delta and we were going to be bush camping for two nights there. I actually liked bush camping and being under a blanket of stars at night with nothing around. It was so peaceful and quiet. We helped the guides bring all of the cooking stuff, tents, and sleeping bags to where we were staying, which was among a cluster of trees. There were elephant feces in huge fibrous chunks all around the camp, evidence that they were definitely around. The guides went to set up a fire and then showed us the bush toilet, which was a hole in the ground behind a group of trees. When someone needed to use the toilet, we were supposed to bring the shovel with us that was sticking out in the ground nearby. If the shovel was gone, that would alert everyone that someone was using the toilet. At least it was cleaner than a public toilet.

After everything was set up, the main guide, named J.D., explained that there were several activities we could do on our own. J.D. was missing some teeth and spoke in a funny way that made me giggle a little bit. He also spoke *very* slowly. It seemed like five years had passed by the time he got around to finish explaining what he wanted to say. The activities included swimming in the Delta (at a designated spot because there were freshwater crocs in other parts) or going on a bush walk or *makoro* ride at 4:30 later that day. It was only around 10 A.M. so we had the whole day before those activities.

I decided to take a dip in the Delta which was actually a lot colder than I thought. The day was searing hot and the sun was so strong. Little black fish could be seen in the reddish tinted water and the mud was squishy and cool beneath my feet. After a quick swim, I spent the rest of the day lazing about and trying to get out of the sun. I read a book in the shade under a large tree until it was time to go on the sunset walk.

There were only five of us for the sunset walk with a guide by the name of Mixture. He called himself Mix for short. He was extremely tall, like a basketball player and spoke even slower than J.D. He said "yes" like "yah" and was extremely knowledgeable about all the plants and the landscape.

"Yah. Eef you see an eleofant, leepard, please leesin to me. (Pause). Yah. They are not close but eef you see one, please don't roon. Yah."

There were definitely elephants and zebras around, as well as hippos and antelope by the looks of various piles of excrement in the bush. There were also tons of huge holes dug into the earth by aardvarks (anteaters). The dangerous snakes were around of course as well, like the Mozambique spitting cobra and the black mamba. I hoped that they would continue to stay out of sight.

The landscape was very flat and covered with white sand. On top of that sandy soil grew various green trees, shrubs, and tall grasses. Mix knew about the landscape well and described the various properties of some of the plants that the San Bushman used to heal themselves with for a variety of illnesses. We saw a pack of zebras in the distance that looked at us curiously until they decided that we were not a threat and then went back to grazing, their noses to the ground like a metal detector. I almost tripped over a rib bone of an elephant and then realized that nearly the whole skeleton was there.

"Theese one died oof an eelness. Yah," Mix explained.

He also explained about hunting game drives in which tourists paid a lot of money to hunt a lion, zebra, elephant, etc. He said that it was regulated by the government and that only a few numbers of animals were killed this way per year. For example, five lions a year were killed in Zimbabwe for the same hunting game drives. Mix said that it cost a lot of money to hunt these animals, like 300,000 U.S.D., but in 2014 a new law was going to be passed by the

Botswana government to make it illegal to do hunting game drives. Here was another new reason to like Botswana. Mix said they usually used old animals for the hunts and the hunter tourist would hire a tracker and they would spend a couple of days tracking the animal and then shoot it. It sounded cruel to me since the animal clearly didn't have a chance out. Also, I had heard a rumor that some of those hunting game drives were set up. The hunter tourist and tracker would "track" the animal for two days and then someone would purposely place the animal somewhere that the tracker knew about. Then, the tracker would "lead" the hunter to the spot and suddenly chance upon the animal.

In some cases, Mix said that the proceeds of the hunting game drives went back into the communities which surprised me. Not all of the proceeds, but some of it. Also, he said that this animal hunt game drive was also a way to control animal populations. However, I knew that lions were quickly diminishing in population so I wasn't sure how that was controlling the population of that particular animal, but perhaps it was true with some of the others.

We continued on our way, watching birds like egrets and hawks hunting over the vast landscape. We continued on until the most glorious sunset caught my eye and the sky filled with red and orange like a flame. With the colors framed against the backdrop of African trees and shrubs, it was a masterpiece of art. The clouds even seemed in awe of it, since they stopped moving and were suspended in the air, their edges rimmed with an intense color. It was the most fantastic show that nature had ever put on.

Chapter Thirty-One

"Okavango Delta"

The next morning I found myself up at the crack of dawn and soon on a bush walk. We took the *makoros* into the Delta, just as the early morning sun hit the water with a soft light. It was quiet and peaceful, with only the sound of the lapping of water against the side of the *makoro*. We split up into groups and I was put into a group with a young man named Stuart who would be our guide. The walk lasted two hours and we walked through the long grass of the open savannah along the Delta. He pointed out various trees used for healing purposes by the San bushman. I was sorry that the bush walk wasn't as good as the previous day's walk with Mix, but we did see a painted reed frog. It seemed to me like the smallest frog in the world, about the size of two of my thumbnails. It was white with red spots and was really cute, until it jumped at me and I had no idea where it had landed. For all I knew it could have been hiding in my bag.

We met everyone else back at the *makoros*. Some of the other groups had seen an elephant carcass that still had the skin on it and had been decaying for about three months. Back at the camp, a couple of the local ladies taught us how to make woven bracelets out of reeds. They cut strips in the reeds which had been dried out in the sun. Some of the pieces had been dyed in colors of brown, black, and purple. I was able to interweave the colored reeds with the plain ones to make a kind of checkered pattern. The women were also selling bracelets and woven baskets as well for about four dollars each. Since I had made a bracelet with one of the ladies I decided to buy one as well. They were beautiful bracelets, the best I had seen so far in Africa.

The rest of the day passed by lazily. The heat of the day peaked and then waned. Five o'clock came and went and we were soon on the *makoros* again and gliding towards another glorious sunset. The water was quiet and I simply absorbed the environment. We came upon a large channel of water and I heard the familiar snort of a hippo suddenly emerging from the water. He looked at us as we hid behind the reeds with only the top of his head and eyes poking out of the water. He was by himself, probably one of the hippos who had been kicked out of the group and who was now lonely and angry. He gave a few more snorts and we turned around because the guides said that it was a warning that he wanted us to go away and leave him alone.

As we made our way back through the reeds and narrow waterways to the camp, we arrived just in time for another stunning show of nature in the form of an awe-inspiring sunset. This time, not only did the clouds stop moving, but they also began to assemble themselves into various forms. I could have sworn the clouds were morphing into shapes of African animals. I could point out the big five in the sky. I wondered if this was some practical joke played by the heavens but no, the clouds really were in the shape of animals...an elephant, a rhino, and a giraffe was clear to see. Perhaps my mind was playing tricks on me. But I didn't think so.

Later that evening after dinner, all the guides led us in some of their country's songs in beautiful voices. The group harmonized and one person sang over the others in a complimentary song and all together, their voices floated to the star-filled sky above. They made the "hmmm" sound and a deep "oh" sound a lot and it was probably the best cultural dance and song combo I had ever heard. Part of it was because they all looked like they were having so much fun doing it. Also, the entire group was blessed with good dance moves and fabulous voices. Mix in particular got really into it, with froggy dances that had him hopping up and down. It wasn't long before we joined him and danced the night away under the dark African star-studded sky.

***

The next morning we departed the Delta, trying to appreciate the last ride in the *makoros* and the way that the lily flowers were reflected on the water. On the way, I chatted with my *makoro* guide, Bothle.

"No kids," he explained in broken English but smiled and pointed to another one of the guides, a middle-aged woman named Lizzy. "My lady friend," he said, smiling. "Before, no lady guides. Only man. Now lady guides. It is happier."

Apparently, it had only been recently that the company had hired females to be *makoro* guides in the Delta, as previously it had been all males. Bothle said that in the high season, he was busy almost every day taking people out into the Delta but during the low season, he might only take people out a couple of days a week.

Once we had arrived back to where we would get out of the *makoros*, I tipped him about ten dollars.

"This big money to me. Thank you," he said.

I was rather embarrassed because it wasn't that much money but he seemed to be really happy with it so I was happy if he was happy.

"You nice quiet girl. I like this. You respect African culture. Thank you."

It was a nice and unexpected thing for him to say. Somehow the way he said it brought tears to my eyes. We said our goodbyes and I wished him luck. I believed Bothle was in his early fifties. He was a rather old man in Botswana, considering the life expectancy was only 27 due to the AIDS epidemic. I was sure if he had gotten this far, he would live a long life.

We hopped in the four-wheel drive that would take us back to the Sepia Hotel. It had been an amazing experience in the Delta and I was glad I had done it. Back at the hotel I ordered lunch from a very funny young lady waitress who decided that she liked my woven bag from Zimbabwe very much.

"This will look very good with one of my dresses, sister," she said, running her fingers over the bag. "Please give it to me."

"Sorry but I had to look really hard for that bag and I don't think I will be giving it away."

"Okay, okay. I make compromise wich you. Paint my nails," she said, motioning to some nail polish that someone else at the table was using.

So with the girl's permission to use her nail polish, I painted the waitress's nails before her boss caught her. I had to say the waitress sure knew how to make a deal.

Chapter Thirty-Two

"Tsodilo Hills and the San Bushman Paintings"

The next morning we left bright and early from the Sepia Hotel to head to Tsodilo Hills, where the San Bushman rock paintings from 3000 years ago were still visible. Tsodilo is a UNESCO World Heritage Site located in northwestern Botswana, about six miles from the Kalahari Desert. The exact age of the paintings there was not known, although some are thought to be more than 20,000 years old. The hills contained 500 individual sites representing thousands of years of human habitation. In total, there were about 4,500 rock paintings on the hills.

Along the way, we passed the edge of the Kalahari Desert. The San Bushmen have lived in the Kalahari for 20,000 years as hunter-gatherers. Bushmen rarely drink water; they get most of their water requirements from plant roots and desert melons found on or under the desert floor. These Bushmen lived in huts built from local materials—the frame is made of branches, and the roof is thatched with long grass. It was amazing to me how humans could adapt to so many environments; we really were very adaptable creatures.

Tsodilo Hills was a place of religious and spiritual significance to the San people of the Kalahari. They believed the hills were a resting place for the spirits of the deceased and that these spirits will cause misfortune and bad luck if anyone hunts or causes death near the hills. The San people believed these hills to be the site of first Creation. I wanted to make sure that I didn't so much as step on an insect while walking around. The last thing I wanted were ancestral spirits of the San Bushman after me. Even it if was only an insect.

It was late in the afternoon and extremely hot when we arrived to Tsodilo hills. Botswana was the flattest country I had ever seen and to see these rocky hills rise up out of the flatness was really surprising. We met our guides who would take us up the rock hills to see the paintings. My guide's was named Flora and she was really knowledgeable about everything regarding Botswana. We spoke about the diamond trade, since Botswana was the largest exporter of diamonds in the world.

"Diamonds are not sold in Botswana and if someone is caught selling them, they will be put in jail," she explained to me.

"So what you are saying is that Botswana has all these diamonds but no one in Botswana has a diamond?" I exclaimed, surprised.

"Yes," she replied. "They are all exported. This is good for us. Botswana makes a lot of money from the exports so we can send our kids to public school for free. We have social welfare programs in place for poor people."

From what Flora was saying, it sounded like Botswana was setting an example for the rest of Africa in their education and social welfare policies.

Flora also explained that HIV retroviral drugs were free in Botswana to those suffering from the disease, but lots of people refused to believe they had HIV and therefore did not take the drugs or get seen by a doctor. Flora had already lost several friends to the disease. She also said that some people preferred to drink alcohol instead of taking the drugs because you weren't supposed to be drinking when on antiretroviral drugs. Botswana had such a high epidemic of AIDS, it was estimated that one in three people had it.

Flora was thirty and she had one son and was thinking about having another. The thing I couldn't get over about Flora was that her skin was absolutely flawless, no wrinkles, no spots, nothing. In fact, most of the African women and men I had seen so far looked really young for their age and their skin didn't seem to wrinkle much. I knew for a fact that many of the African people with this kind of luminous skin were not using $600 creams on their skin or going for facials every week. It was definitely a genetic thing. For this, they were certainly lucky.

We began huffing and puffing our way up the rocky hill and along the way saw several different paintings of animals such as rhino, giraffe, and buffalo in strokes of red and white. The art was described as a "human diary" and I couldn't think of a more appropriate word.

"There are no more rhino in this area, but there were rhinos here 3000 years ago when the paintings we are now seeing had first been made," Flora explained.

The red pigments in some of the paintings were ground mainly from iron oxide, which were powdered and mixed with animal fat to form an adhesive paste. The white pigment came from silica, powdered quartz and white clays, and was by nature less adhesive than the red pigments. For this reason white paintings survived only in sheltered locations, such as well-protected caves. Both pigments were applied using sticks, the artists' fingers, and brushes made from animal hair. Seeing these ancient paintings was really amazing, especially since the artists' canvas was nature itself. We were literally walking through an open-air, completely natural art gallery with a year-round exhibition.

Most of the rock paintings reflected people's relationship with nature. The majority were realistic portrayals of hunters, giraffes, elephants, rhinos, etc. Common themes included the roles of men and women, hunting scenes, and natural medicine. Dry climate and sheltered granite overhangs had preserved many of the more recent paintings. I saw both red paintings and white paintings along with depictions of animals, especially rhino and antelope.

Flora informed me that there were leopards in the hills but the guides had never seen them as they were so hard to spot (no pun intended). I stopped along the way back to wrap my arms around a huge baobab tree. Its bark looked like dark grey steel. The baobab is the largest tree in Africa.

"I love baobab juice," Flora said. "But I hate mopane worms."

We finished the hike, dripping in sweat. It really was steaming hot, almost unbearably so. Back at the camp, a few hours later, a wind storm blew over us, knocking down all the tents. I went straight to bed. There was nothing better than falling asleep to the sound of the howling wind. Unfortunately there were inchworms everywhere and they were definitely larger than one inch long. It was a good thing I wasn't scared of bugs. For anyone that is, well, I wouldn't recommend camping in Africa. They were all over the tent and were trying to get in. I just hoped that if they did make it inside, that they didn't bite. I was more than willing to share but biting was one thing I just couldn't tolerate.

Chapter Thirty-Three

"Etosha National Park-the Underdog Wins"

We left Tsodilo Hills the next morning, as the dawn began to creep up over the horizon. We were heading to Namibia. Our first night would be at a bush camp and then we would make our way to Etosha National Park for some game driving for two days before heading to Swakopmund.

The immigration process at the Namibian border took ages but the officers sat at a very nice looking immigration desk with a huge wooden carving of all the various animals that you could find in Namibia. It was really interesting because you could tell the wealth of the African countries that you entered by the quality of the entrance or departure forms that you had to fill out at immigration. So if you compared the forms from Namibia to those of

Malawi, you would definitely see that they were better off. It was a good indication, that's all.

Namibia is one of the youngest countries in Africa and is squeezed between the Kalahari Desert and the South Atlantic. The reason that it is a young country in terms of colonialism is due to the fact that Namibia has one of the world's most inhospitable coastlines called the Skeleton Coast and therefore, no one wanted to attempt to explore the land. The first European visitors were Portuguese mariners seeking a route to the Indies in the late 15th century, but they didn't get too far due to the inhospitable terrain.

Luckily, however, settlers had paved the way for us and we were well on our way into Namibia. We stopped in Rundu just over the border for a very late lunch and to pick up some supplies. Our tour guide had told us to be careful in Namibia and South Africa because there were a lot of pickpocketing activities and opportunistic muggings because the gap between rich and poor was so wide. Some people in the last group that she had been in charge of had had their money pickpocketed from them in the supermarket. I knew that some tensions endured between various social and racial groups but it was not confined to black/white relations as Namibia's ethnic groups were extremely varied.

I picked up a sandwich from the supermarket and a large grapefruit. In Africa, when you bought fruit, you had to have it weighed and priced by someone before you brought it to the checkout.

"What is this?" the young guy weighing and pricing my grapefruit asked.

He had no idea what kind of fruit it was and therefore sauntered off to ask someone. Then another person came and no one knew what kind of fruit it was so I had to explain what a grapefruit was, which was kind of funny because the item was in *their* supermarket. Perhaps no one ever bought grapefruit in Namibia.

We hopped back on the truck and arrived at the bush camp in the evening, just as the sun was setting. The bush camp was set up next to a giant baobab tree that was even on major maps in Namibia. It was *that* big.

***

The next morning we woke up at the pale light of dawn again. This particular day we would be game driving in Etosha National Park in our overland truck and also staying at a campsite in the park. Etosha meant "great white place of dry water". This name is inspired from the vast greenish-white Etosha Pan, an immense, flat, saline desert that, for a few days each

year, is converted by the rains into a shallow lagoon
teeming with flamingos and pelicans.

We arrived at Etosha around 10 A.M. for the
game drive. The campsite was 50 miles into the park
so just getting there was a game drive in itself. Along
the way, I spotted long-legged giraffes strolling
across the flat-as-a-pancake sun bleached land. It was
like seeing a painting come to life. There were salt
pans and a sea of white in the distance. The giraffes
were curious about us and stopped to stare. One bent
down to get a drink from a waterhole and it bent its
legs at such a funny angle that I had to laugh. Its legs
bent the opposite angle as ours do when we bend
them so it looked like the giraffes' legs were broken.

Besides the giraffes there were grasslands
dotted with gemsbok, a really rare type of antelope
that I had never seen before in my life. I wondered
where they had been hiding my entire life. They were

the most beautiful I had seen, with muscular grey bodies and black markings. They had long faces like a wildebeest with white and black markings and long, straight black antlers. They were elegant but strong-looking at the same time. I only saw them in pairs as well, one male and one female, not in big groups like other antelopes. They were mainly desert-dwelling creatures and did not depend on drinking water to supply their physiological needs, which is why the Etosha salt pans were perfect for them. Again, they were another example of a very adaptable species. For every place on earth that we think is uninhabitable to any life forms, there always is something that can survive there.

In addition, there were also black-faced impala, a rare breed. They had almost reached extinction at one point and had been moved to Etosha and had then thrived and multiplied. We saw two of the males fighting over a female, their heads locked together in each other's horns, pushing and knocking into each other. I could tell it was going to be a long fight.

There were the usual gazelle and impala grouped together on the grasslands, always munching. The landscape was beautiful, with a huge and endless blue sky dotted with cotton candy clouds over vast unbroken plains and salt pans. Occasional trees dotted the landscape along with the random waterhole. Zebras of a lighter color (Burchell's zebra) could be seen in groups and even *they* seemed to blend into the landscape. The colors of individual animals often stand out but when you put them in the grasslands, even zebras and giraffes blend in. It was sometimes hard to spot things. Jackals moved in and out of the grass and they looked like small coyotes. They were easily scared and kept looking around to see if anything was behind them.

We stopped when two African elephants walked toward us on the dirt road that we were driving on. They were huge and covered in mud (they used it as sunscreen), flapping their enormous ears as they walked toward us. There were a few females with their young ones and they all looked like they were smiling as they crossed the road. I saw one of them tear a huge branch off a tree like it was absolutely nothing. Elephants were rather destructive to trees and landscape because they simply plowed through everything because, well, they *could*. The damage they had caused to people's land in Botswana was immense.

Further on down the road there was a huge waterhole filled with hundreds of pink flamingoes. Flamingoes were really skittish; they would fly off as soon as anything got remotely close to them. They also clearly liked being in a huge group. Flamingos are very social birds; they live in colonies whose population can number in the thousands. The large colonies are believed to serve three purposes: avoiding predators, maximizing food intake, and using nesting sites more efficiently. There were also corrie bustards, hornbills, African fish eagles, and hawks.

We arrived at the campsite around lunch to eat and have a swim in the pool before heading out for an evening game drive. The evening game drive was cooler in temperature, of course, than the midday one so I was looking forward to seeing some different animals that might come out in the evening. The endless landscape was so flat that you could see for miles. A single acacia tree on the horizon only made it seem more African. It wasn't long before I saw a couple of spotted hyenas. They blended so well with the environment that it was hard to spot them. They seemed to be scavenging for food, although the truth is that they are better hunters than lions.

Further down the road, a highlight of the game drive popped into our line of vision. It was a black rhino, grazing on a clump of grass. Black rhinos were nearly extinct and very rare to see. It was on its own and we stopped the truck so we could quietly observe it as it came closer. At times, it would look at us curiously but perhaps it could smell us rather than see us. Rhinos had a keen sense of smell but were really nearsighted so it most likely didn't see us. Every once in a while it would jump and shake as though it were spooked. Perhaps it sensed our presence. After some time passed, it scuttled off into the bush.

The animals weren't the only awe-inspiring thing I saw. The infinite sky was motionless above. It seemed limitless, as high as it was wide. Back at the

campsite, we were told there was a waterhole that was

lit up at night by floodlights and we could sit and look

for animals at night. By the time I arrived there after

dark, the sky was lit up with a zigzag pattern of

lightening streaks. For a moment the sky would be

ink black and still. Then thunder clouds would clap

their giant hands so loudly that the sky seemed to

split. Lightening would appear in the form of streaks

of ghostly green light that flickered and danced across

the sky. This was an incredible show by Mother

Nature herself and I had a front row seat. And the

tickets were free.

***

The next morning everything was flooded. It

had stormed all through the night and I woke up on a

cold and soggy sleeping mat, which I have to say, is one of the least pleasant ways to wake up. I poked my head outside the tent and could see that the tent was sitting or rather, nearly floating in water that was well above my ankles. Not even a waterproof tent could survive this. Trust me when I say that it is not fun to go camping in torrential rain. Everything in the tent was wet. I began to pack up my soggy items; knowing with a sinking heart that they weren't going to dry and they would start to stink.

Luckily, something cheered me up not long after we set out. On the game drive that morning, it just so happened that this time, we chanced upon six lionesses with their baby cubs. They were almost invisible and blended in so well with the golden savannah grass on which they were laying on. They had just killed something that looked like it was once a gazelle and were each taking turns gnawing a huge bloody chunk of meat. While the adults were taking turns eating, the cubs played nearby, tumbling together in wrestling matches with each other. When they were done playing, they went to their mothers, who would give them a quick bath. Out of the corner of my eye however, I saw some movement in the grass. It was a jackal, no bigger than a small dog. I could already tell that it had its eye on the lionesses' fresh kill and it was looking to scavenge some meat. I couldn't believe the audacity of the jackal…didn't it know that it was veering way to close to creatures that would rip it to shreds in a matter of seconds? The jackal crept cautiously around the lions. I wasn't sure what he was thinking…I mean he couldn't have thought that he could take the lionesses' meat right from under their noses did he? Or perhaps he wished to join them in their feast by becoming part of the main course. But I didn't think so.

Suddenly one of the lionesses saw the jackal creeping closer. The jackal hadn't noticed that he had indeed been dangerously spotted by a fierce predator. He continued stupidly staring at the meat. The lioness crouched down and slinked toward him, her ears perked and belly to the ground. Seconds seemed like minutes and I thought the jackal was about to become kill number two that day for the lionesses. Just as the lioness was about to pounce, the jackal realized that he was about to become no more and raced away. The lioness watched him run away and must have decided that he wasn't worth the chase. Perhaps the gazelle was enough to fill their bellies for the moment.

Suddenly, a roar of a male lion could be heard in the distance. The lionesses all stood up, their ears perked. The jackal was forgotten about. Quickly, the lionesses gathered up the cubs and left the scene quickly, running away from the direction of the roar.

It was clear that the roar of the male lion in the distance did not belong to the male lion that was a member of their own group. It was the roar of a male lion looking to take over a pride and kick the other male out. These new lions were most likely nomadic lions that had been kicked out of their own pride as soon as they had become adolescents by the alpha male of their own pride. They were now roaming around looking for a new pride this time, and one which they would be the leaders of. And the sad thing is that when a new leader arrives in a pride, he kills the cubs of that pride. No wonder the lionesses hightailed it out of there, the cubs' lives were in danger.

We soon saw these two male lions. They were pure blonde, full of muscle, and sauntered through the long tall grass with confidence. They looked like they had just grown in their manes because they were short, a pure blonde color, and looked soft and fluffy. They strode purposely through the grass and paused every now and again to sniff the air. They were looking for the pride of lionesses that had just run off and they had nearly sniffed them out. They soon found where they had been laying down and sniffed all along the ground, their noses like metal detectors looking for something. They hadn't found what they were looking for but they had come close. They walked off into the distance, still pausing to sniff the air every so often. We watched them until they became specks. The last thing I saw before we drove off was the jackal, who had snuck quietly back to where the lionesses had left their lunch. He had managed to get his piece of leftover meat after all.

Chapter Thirty-Four

"Cheetah Fever in Namibia"

Cheetah Park was where we would be seeing cheetahs up close and personal. It was really hard to see cheetahs in the wild as well as leopards. I was ready to see a spotted cat. We would be seeing two groups of cheetahs, tame ones and wild ones. Cheetahs were considered a pest in Namibia and farmers shot them when they attacked their cattle. Cheetah Park was owned by one particular farmer who had tame cheetahs running around his farm.

"I was a former cheetah hater that had shot a cheetah that had been attacking my cattle. But then I saw that the cheetah was a female who had a few cubs. So I kept the cubs and raised them like domesticated cats. The cats go in and out of the house when they please," he explained.

The farmer had several dogs and grandkids on the farm that had also grown up with the cheetahs. I couldn't imagine growing up with such a pet. It would certainly be something cool to bring to "show and tell" day at school.

On the other part of his land, he had a very large enclosure/park dedicated to wild cheetahs that had been dropped off by other farmers who had considered them pests because they were messing around with cattle. So it was a good alternative for cheetahs to be saved from a gun. The wild cheetahs had plenty of space to roam freely and the tame cheetahs were happy to be tame. The cheetah can run faster than any other land animal, as fast as 70 to 75 mph in short bursts covering distances up to 1,600 feet, and has the ability to accelerate from 0 to over 62 mph in five seconds.

First it was time to see the tame cheetahs who turned out to be, well, tame! They roamed around with the farmer's dogs and they purred like housecats when you rubbed their neck and head.

"Don't wear sunglasses while you are with the cheetahs," the farmer warned. "They don't like their own reflection."

I wondered who had learned that lesson the hard way. The cats were so gorgeous with their big eyes and spots that I didn't see why they weren't vainer and couldn't stand their own reflection.

One thing that I simply could not get over was the way they purred. They seemed to be particularly pleased to be petted on their neck. I could have been petting my cat Minnie at home for all the difference that I could see in the way they purred. Their purrs were deep and rumbled, like the faint sound of a motor. When they stood, they were up to my hip and were long and lean, with small heads and broad chests. There were about four adult cheetahs and one baby in total. They wandered around leisurely, posing under trees and on top of tractors like supermodels. For lunch, we watched them dig into some donkey meat that still had hair on it. Perhaps it was the remains of the three-legged donkey I had seen at the Maasai camp in Tanzania. I was pretty sure that was pretty much what his fate was going to be; cheetah food.

There was also a campsite on the property and so it wasn't far to go to set up our tents. After doing so, we hopped in the back of a small pickup to go on a game drive to see the wild cheetahs with the son of the owner. The owners had German ancestry, like many other white Namibians. In fact, many of the signs and town names in Namibia were German.

We were soon through the gates of a very large enclosure/game park. It was so big I couldn't even tell it was an enclosure. It wasn't long until we saw four cheetahs running toward us. There wasn't much protection with just being in the back of a very low pickup with a couple of railings so as they got closer, I got a little bit nervous. Of course, you could instantly tell the difference between the tame cheetahs and the wild ones. A couple of them hissed at us and did a fake pounce move on us along with swiping their paw in our direction. They were all salivating heavily. They were so close, only about seven feet away. They paced in circles and made noises at each other that sounded as though they were having a private conversation. They swiped at each other as well. They were mean and nasty little buggers compared to the tame ones who loved to be petted.

What a difference their environments had been on their behavior!

I nearly choked in disbelief when I saw the owner's son get out of the truck with only a small stick and a piece of meat. He was actually going to feed the cheetahs and face them head on. I wasn't sure if he was actually sane or if he was numb to the dangers of wild animals. The cheetahs hissed at him and swiped but didn't actually make contact because it was clear that they knew they were about to get fed. The guy threw a huge piece of meat into the air and one of the cheetahs leapt and grabbed it with both paws in mid-air. Another one with battle scars and wound marks on his face growled at the one who caught it and they briefly fought over the piece of meat. Even though the other cheetah caught the meat, I thought it was in his best interest to give the meat to old scarface. They hissed and swiped at each other and scarface managed to get the meat in the end.

After feeding that particular group of cheetahs, we moved further into the field until we found another group who the man fed in the same manner; all the while the cats were hissing, salivating, and jumping to catch the meat. It really was a sight to behold.

The sky was darkening and thunder rumbled in the distance. The smell of rain hung heavy in the air. It was time to get back to the tent before another downpour. Unfortunately, just as I was walking with all of my things to the tent it started to pour. And I mean torrential rains as though the heavens had burst. I ran towards the tent and at that moment, my flip flop decided to break so I had to run barefoot which slowed me down substantially. Not only that, there seemed to be a field mine of acacia thorns that had fallen from the surrounding trees onto the path. Not the best place to run through barefoot. I wanted to scream as thorns poked into my skin as I walked. Did I mention that camping and torrential rain just don't mix?

The only thing that consoled me later that evening, was a reduction in the rainfall and also that we were having gemsbok for dinner. It was from the really big solid antelope that I had seen the previous day in Etosha. The meat was really good; it looked exactly like a beef steak and almost tasted like one too. I thought it was delicious. It was hard to be both beautiful and delicious but the gemsbok had pulled it off to perfection.

Chapter Thirty-Five

"The Namib Desert"

We set off for Swakopmund, a city on the northwestern Skeleton coast of Namibia, for our fifth early morning in a row the following day. I couldn't believe that Christmas was just around the corner. I would be in the desert, bush camping in Spitzkoppe and surrounded by rock formations. It was certainly going to be a Christmas I would never forget.

The rain had ebbed and we were all greeted with a huge rainbow that stretched across the sky. This was a full rainbow, vibrant with colors. We were back on the road soon enough and by mid-morning we had entered the Namib Desert, the oldest desert in the world. The Namib is almost completely uninhabited by humans except for several small settlements and indigenous pastoral groups, including the Ovahimba and Obatjimba Herero in the north, and the Topnaar Nama in the central region. The Nama word "namib," which inspired the name of the entire country, means "vast dry plain".

The Namib Desert was a flat beige-colored desert with scrub brush here and there and with a range of grey rock mountains that loomed in the background. As we got further into the desert, I could see a lake and then a gorge. But wait, it wasn't really a lake or a gorge. It was a mirage. Continuing on I could see that the scrub brush got less and less until it was just beige colored dirt that looked like it was on its way to becoming sand. This was a desolate place and not a good one to be stuck in. The sky was vast as usual and not a soul was in sight. There were no huts and no people. It was a vast contrast from Kenya, whose fields and roads were always populated with people. This place was deserted, no pun intended.

Mirages continued to punctuate the horizon. Mountains in the distance became islands in the midst of the shimmering mirage. This was one sparse population and I wouldn't want to be lost in it.

Further down we stopped at a stand in the middle of the desert, where Herero and Himba women were selling bracelets. These were the tribal people of Namibia. They were both from the same tribe but had split up into two factions, which was evident in the way that they were clothed. The Herero woman was dressed in a kind of pioneer dress that would have been popular with women in Europe or America in the early 1900s. She also wore a kind of square shaped hat. The only way to describe it would be to say if you wrapped up an empty small-sized pizza box from Dominoes in a scarf, raised it on a little stand within the scarf and put it on your head.

The Herero used to dress like the Himbas (with almost no clothes) but the colonialists who had come to Namibia from Europe had decided that it wasn't appropriate for women to walk around naked and had therefore made them put on some clothes. But the Himba hadn't listened and had gone off on their own, splitting the group into two factions. The other woman at this lone stand in the middle of the desert was a Himba lady. She wore almost nothing except a short brown skirt made of animal skin, ankle bracelets, and a kind of suspenders which criss-crossed in front of her chest. She was bare-chested and her hair and skin were covered with what looked like mud but was really a mixture of ochre, butter, and bush herbs. This dyed her skin a burnt-orange hue, and served as a natural sun block and insect repellent. The woman was one of a group of Himba of no more than 50,000 that continue to live like they have been doing for generations.

We continued on through the desert until we reached the Atlantic Coast, which really existed and was not a mirage (I tested it by dipping my toe in the water). This was the part of Namibia that made up the formidable Skeleton Coast. Low and behold, before my very eyes, was a sunken ship in the sea, with nothing but its rusted shell sticking out of the water. More than a thousand shipwrecks litter the Skeleton Coast and this was just one of many. Most of the wrecks had been caused by a thick fog that occurred when a cold current hits a warm one. This formed a thick mist that caused the ships to crash into rocks and sandy coastal shallows. Early Portuguese sailors called it the "sands of hell" as once a ship washed ashore, the fate of the crew was sealed.

We headed to Swakopmund after testing that the water from the Atlantic was real and not a mirage. Swakopmund had often been described as being more German than Germany, as its settlers had been German. I had reached the Atlantic and had crossed Africa from coast to coast. It was a great feeling.

Chapter Thirty-Six

"Christmas in the Desert"

After a restful three days in Swakopmund wandering around and going to the beach and local markets, we departed for Spitzkoppe, a series of rock formations in the desert. Spitzkoppe is one of Namibia's most instantly recognizable landmarks and rises like a tower in southern Damaraland. This was where I would be spending my first African Christmas. We would be bush camping for two nights there and I was sure it was going to be one of the more interesting Christmas holidays that I had experienced.

We arrived at the amazing red rock monoliths in the early afternoon. They were huge rock formations, many of them like smooth balls piled on top of each other. It reminded me of Uluru and the

Olgas in Australia. Some had smooth, sheer faces of red rock while other parts were just a huge pile of medium to small-sized boulders.

We set up camp at the foot of a large smooth rock mountain with smaller boulders piled on the top like marbles. It was a stunning location. The sky was a bright blue, the ground was white sand and surrounding us were giant red rocks reaching to the sky. It looked like we were on Mars. There were a few acacia trees here and there so I set up my tent under one of them to get some relief from the intense heat of the sun.

Along with a few others, I decided to climb some rocks. Some of them were really challenging, requiring you to jump across deep ravines and watch your step very carefully. It was fantastic and after crossing over one rock formation, we moved onto another. There were snakes in the area so we had to be careful, not to mention scorpions, lots of thorny bushes, and piles of small feces in the form of pellets. The feces pellets belonged to rock dassies, a small mammal which looked like a guinea pig that lived among the rocks in large groups. The views were stunning from the rock formations, of endless desert that was so flat that there was just a single straight line on the horizon. Shrub brush dotted the landscape and I wondered how anything could grow in such a dry and intense heat. But there were obviously species who thrived here.

Down by the truck, a fire was started and dinner was beginning to be cooked. We sat around chatting about Christmas and then ate our dinner and roasted marshmallows. A blanket of stars was laid above us and they seemed so brilliant that I could touch them with my hand. Needless to say, I didn't even need to use a flashlight. The stars provided

enough light.

***

The next morning I woke up and it was

Christmas! It didn't really feel like Christmas since I

wasn't from the Southern Hemisphere, where it was

hot on Christmas Day. I wondered what all the people

I loved who weren't with me were doing. I was

handling Christmas in the desert better than I thought.

I had expected to be homesick throughout the day but

somehow, Africa had fooled me into believing that

there was no Christmas. I am the ultimate Christmas

lover. I start putting up decorations after

Thanksgiving and listening to Christmas songs a

month before Christmas. I love the traditions, the

food, the presents, the parties. But I had survived so far by simply being in denial. It worked a treat.

Our tour leaders were preparing a big breakfast for us, in addition to Christmas lunch/dinner. Breakfast was really good, with sausages, bacon, beans, eggs, toast, and juice. After breakfast we decided to go rock climbing. An American couple in our group had rock-climbing gear as they were avid rock climbers and had found bolts on the side of a rock face about five minutes from camp. About nine people had a try at rock climbing. The rock face was actually really hard to climb and I only made about 60 percent of the climb before calling it quits. It was really much harder than it looked.

After rock climbing we had some snacks and sat around for a while until it was time for dinner. To pull off a Christmas dinner on a gas cooker is a pretty big feat but our tour leaders pulled it off. On offer

were chicken, rosemary lamb, gravy, potatoes,

carrots, cranberry sauce, and all the condiments that

came with Christmas dinners. We went on another

rock scramble after dinner, up the formations, and

then watched the most amazing purple and pink

sunset over the desert. That was probably the best

present I could have received on Christmas. I had to

really remember that sometimes, the best presents

cost no money at all.

Chapter Thirty-Seven

"Dune 45"

I was sad to leave Spitzkoppe after Christmas, it had been a great place to spend it. The next destination however, was an exciting one. We were heading to the famous Namibian sand dunes or more specifically, Namib-Naukluft Park which is best known for Sossusvlei, a huge pan set amid infamous towering red dunes. The dunes are part of the Namib Desert, which stretches more than 1,242 miles along the coast from Oliphants River in South Africa all the way to southern Angola. The dunes can reach as high as 1000 feet and they are a part of one of the oldest and driest ecosystems on earth. The landscape was constantly changing due to the wind forever altering the dunes' shapes.

The drive into the national park was stunning, with golden grassland stretching to the horizon and framed with rock mountains with sharp edges. There were lots of ostriches on the grasslands. Some were close and some were far away. The ones that were far away simply looked like a lot of black specks amongst the golden grasslands. I couldn't believe it that within a week or so, my African trip would be finished and these sights would be just a memory. It was hard to believe how time had passed that quickly. Looking back on the start of the trip, I thought it seemed like such a long time ago.

As we got closer to the sand dunes, the mountains turned from rock into sand and the color became a burnt red. We were on a road through a flat and dry valley with graceful dunes of red sand on either side. It was beautiful scenery and the dunes rose into sharp crests. The sand dunes seemed like they were two colors, one of dark brown and the other of golden red, depending on what side was bathed in sunlight and what side was in the shade.

We had two hours to climb the most famous of them all, Dune 45. Its name came from the fact that it was at the 45th kilometer (27th mile) of the road that connects the Sesriem gate and Sossusvlei. It stood over 170m tall and was composed of 5 million year old sand that was accumulated by the Orange River from the Kalahari Desert and then blown to Dune 45. So the sand was originally from the Kalahari. It had traveled a long way to get here. I decided to climb barefoot because it was easier. I began the descent up the dune. It was hard work but the sand was as soft as a fine powder under my feet and surprisingly not too hot because my feet sunk into the cooler sand below the surface. It was the color of burnt copper and was also the home to sand lizards and sand beetles. The lizards were amazing, lifting their legs off the sand if it was too hot and rotating their arms and legs if one got too hot. They also dove under the sand to escape from the heat and made beautiful flower-like patterns across the sand, like a vine. The side of the sand dunes was so smooth and in the wind, small swirls of sand danced on top of the smooth surface like mini-whirlpools. The sky was blue and seemed endless above us and the sun shone fiercely in this environment.

I made my way to the top and admired the views of sand dunes stretching endlessly on my right. To my left, there was another view of the sweeping and flat valley below. A single road ran through it like a long black snake and from the top of the dune, the valley looked like a salt pan with various shades of black etched into it. I sat on the top of the dune for a while, taking pictures and admiring the landscape.

To get down, I ran down the steep side of the dune very fast. It felt like flying because it was so steep and it was hard to fall because the sand was a really good support system to fall into. It was a really fun way to get down the sand dune except that towards the bottom, where the sun was shining the most intensely, the sand was piping hot. I hobbled back to the truck and then we were on the road again, this time heading to a bush camp that was nearer to Fish River Canyon, which we would be visiting the following day.

The drive that day was beautiful, with more views of endless desert. I tried to take "photographs" with my mind so I would never forget the sights. There was hardly a soul on the road besides us and a part of me missed waving at so many kids in other African countries. Because the sun wasn't going to go down for a while, the tour leaders decided it was best not to bush camp and instead we stayed at an organized campsite. It wasn't safe to bush camp before dark and with bush camps we had to get up at the crack of dawn so no one spotted us. It wasn't safe to be driving at night in Africa in general either. Although I really enjoyed bush-camping, I was happy that we were at a campsite because it meant I could take a shower, have an earlier dinner than expected, and not have to get up so early. All in all a winning situation.

***

Fish River Canyon was the destination of the day and was the second biggest canyon in the world after the Grand Canyon in the U.S.A. It featured a gigantic ravine, in total about 100 miles long, up to 16 miles in width, and the inner canyon reached a depth of 1, 804 feet. We drove through more hot, dry, and barren desert until we reached the canyon. On first impression, it did somewhat resemble the Grand Canyon although it had different rock formations. A small, dried up river curled around the bottom of the canyon, like a withered snake. It was extremely hot which was to be expected. I wore a jacket just to protect myself from the sun but after a while, found that I couldn't bear to have it on. The heat bore down on us as we wandered around, the sun beating upon our backs. I imagined myself turning a nice crispy brown in the heat. All I needed was some oil and salt.

After spending a couple of hours wandering around the edges of the canyon, we hopped back in the hot truck and moved towards the Orange River, on the border between South Africa and Namibia. It was getting closer to the end of the trip. We would spend two nights at a nice campsite on the border, with one free day to pack up all of our stuff. It was our last drive day on Jozi, the overland truck, as she wouldn't be crossing the border into South Africa with us. Instead, we would be taking an air-conditioned bus from the border all the way to Cape Town, all in all about a 9-10 hour drive.

I spent the rest of the afternoon gazing out the window and spotting ostrich running through the dry lands. The only punctuation in the long drive was a stop for a much needed cold drink sometime in the afternoon at a convenience store where they sold shoes made of Kudu skin. We made a quick stop at SPAR supermarket right before arriving at the campsite later that day to pick up some items. The SPAR was located in a township on the outskirts of town, where houses made of hay, stone, and sticks could be seen dotting the landscape for miles. A river ran through this part of Namibia, the first water I had seen in this desert land. It was somewhat of an oasis, with desert landscape in the background and trees huddled around the river. It was clear to see why a town had been built here and not anywhere else in the desert. The township was a bit of a shock after being in a higher socioeconomic area of Africa (namely Swakopmund). It was very clear that this was a low-socioeconomic area and we were going back to having our bags checked before entering and exiting the supermarket.

We arrived at a beautiful campsite sometime in the early evening. I had been amazed all throughout the trip by the high quality of the campsites in Africa. This campsite had a pool, a bar, and even a gift shop. It was possible to upgrade to a room for about 50 bucks per person but I only had two nights left in the tent. After all we had been through together in the last three months, I owed the tent at least the next two nights together.

Chapter Thirty-Eight

"Goodbye Namibia"

The time had come to say goodbye to Namibia. I was up at the first glimpse of dawn to get all my stuff loaded onto the bus that would take us to Cape Town. There were places to go and things to see! The air-conditioned bus seemed like an absolute dream compared to the truck. The trucks open sides allowed hot air to flow freely through my hair, which sounded nice in theory but wasn't when you actually had to comb out masses of tangled hair at the end of the day. So, the bus was going to be a nice change.

The first stop of the day was at the Namibian/South African border, where we shuffled through immigration on both sides. Then we hopped aboard another bus on the South African side. It was time to say goodbye to the deserts of Namibia and enter the....wait...deserts of South Africa! From the border down, it was mostly rugged, dry, and dusty desert dotted with scrub brush. It didn't seem like many people lived in these parts, probably for good reason. Along the way, we drove through the Cederberg Mountains, wine farms, and the Oliphants and Orange River valleys.

We reached Cape Town around 5 P.M. and it was a culture-shock to the senses. Big buildings, modern city, trendy people walking around, bars, restaurants, shopping...it was my version of a real city, the first I had seen in Africa that was comparable to modern Western cities.

Cape Town had certainly grown from its original use as a supply station for Dutch ships sailing to Eastern Africa, India, and the Far East. It had been developed by the Dutch East India Company for this sole purpose in the mid-1600s, but over time, Cape

Town was established as the first permanent European settlement in South Africa. The settlement grew slowly during this period, as there was a shortage of labor. This shortage of labor prompted the authorities to import slaves from Indonesia and Madagascar. Many of these slaves became ancestors of the first "cape colored" communities. More time passed and Cape Town quickly grew to be the cultural and economic hub of the Cape Colony. Cape Town today is a multi-cultural city of around 4 million people.

We were staying at a hostel in Cape Town that was in a great location. It was just around the corner from Long Street, the place to be in the city. Long Street had a multitude of restaurants, shops, and bars and everyone was going out for a final group dinner. Once we had checked into our rooms, we managed to quickly get ready. The restaurant was beautiful and despite the sharp wind in Cape Town, I enjoyed sitting in the courtyard of the restaurant over a dinner of warthog ribs and an ostrich burger. I had eaten emu before in Australia but not ostrich, so it was my first time for both kinds of game. The warthog ribs were a dream and I wasn't even a big meat eater. The restaurant gave us wine to share among us as a part of the dinner which was amazing. We laughed and took pictures of our last night together as a group. From here on out everyone was leaving at different times and others had various plans.

After dinner we went to an Irish pub on Long Street where they were playing live covers of popular songs. It was a fun night of singing and dancing away. Our tour leader had told us that Cape Town was quite dangerous and it wasn't safe to walk in groups of less than three or four. So when someone wanted to leave, they couldn't really go home by themselves. I waited until a large enough group of us were ready to go and hoped that we could all save each other from whatever danger lurked outside.

***

After making it back safely the night before, the next morning a few of us decided to just take it easy and walk around Cape Town leisurely. I ended up at the best indoor market *ever* for handmade souvenirs and ended up with carved wooden spoons, woven bracelets, two carved bone bottle openers, and bone chopsticks, along with a few other things for friends and family. Most of the vendors at the market were women from Kenya. Once they had learned that I had visited Kenya, they offered discounts and got excited that I had visited their home country.

"God bless you for going to Kenya," one of them said.

I grabbed lunch at an Ethiopian restaurant inside the market. I always love Ethiopian food because it is so fun to eat. The restaurant staff brings you a bowl and soap to wash your hands before eating. You eat with your hands by using the bread to pick up the small portions of dishes that are artfully placed on top of the very large piece of injera bread. Injera is a kind of traditional Ethiopian sourdough flatbread. It is really soft and spongy. The piece of bread that arrives when you order an Ethiopian dish is literally three times the size of an average person's face. That is one large piece of flatbread! Needless to say I couldn't finish all of it.

The only bad thing about that particular day is that I was feeling absolutely exhausted. Perhaps the full brunt of the trip had finally hit me and I knew it

was coming to an end anyways. Or I had grown unfit.
Either way, I was enjoying spending the day without
any plan and meandering along Long Street. It was
New Year's Eve that night and I was planning to head
out with a few people. I was excited to just take in the
scene and see how the locals celebrated the end of the
year.

I went back to the hostel to get ready and
headed out around 9 P.M. The streets were packed
with people who had come into Cape Town from the
townships. Cape Town is probably the city with the
biggest gap between the rich and the poor. From the
big mansions on the seafront to the townships outside
of the city, it really was a horrendous gap and one that
was the cause of so many crimes in this city.

During the Apartheid Era from 1948 to 1994,
blacks were evicted from properties that were in areas
designated as "white only" and forced to move into

segregated townships. Townships were established by races for the three main non-white race groups (blacks, "coloreds", and Indians). Within the townships today, there are some problems. Most often the homes are built on lands that are not owned by the occupier so they are there illegally. Because they are located illegally, they don't have the proper services needed, such as sewage, electricity, roads, and clean water.

A lot of people from the townships had come in on this particular evening into downtown Cape Town to see a parade that was meant to happen around 10 P.M. It looked like many of them had been on the sidewalks all day and some appeared to be planning to sleep there overnight. The wind on this particular evening was something that I can't even describe. It was fierce and full of strength, nearly blowing me over backwards sometimes. It was so strong that I could lean into it and be supported. I wasn't even sure it was safe to be walking around in this kind of high wind. It reminded me of typhoon season in South East Asia.

It was because of this wind that the parade was cancelled. Instead, the group of us decided to wait until the New Year's Eve countdown on Long Street so we could see the festivities. By the time we walked there it was nearing midnight. The street was absolutely packed with people. Everyone seemed to be in a good mood and were shouting and laughing.

The countdown started and suddenly it was 2013! Horns blew and people kissed and wished each other Happy New Year. My New Year's Eve 2012 had been spent in Las Vegas in a massive crowd of people and my New Year's Eve 2013 was in Cape Town on a crowded street of all places. Who would have known?

I decided that New Year's Eve always had too many expectations associated with it and it was easier to just go with the flow, which was exactly what we were doing. No big parties planned, no hundred dollar tickets to anything…just walking around and feeling the atmosphere. You never know what you can find when you just let it go.

Chapter Thirty-Nine

"The City by the Cape"

After New Year's Eve there were another two and a half days to spend in Cape Town. On New Year's Day, a group of us decided to take the hop-on, hop-off bus around the city. I've seen these in lots of major cities but have always shunned them as being too easy for the hardened traveler that I consider myself to be. However, I was tired after three months of traveling and a hop-on, hop-off open top sightseeing bus sounded like just what the doctor ordered. I really couldn't be bothered to walk around the city as I usually would do, with a map, a pair of good shoes, and a walking tour guide. I was ready to let someone else do the work for me. So for the price of twenty dollars, I did just that.

The hop-on, hop-off sightseeing bus turned out to be the best thing I could have done for myself to really see Cape Town. The day was sunny and warm and it was perfect to be looking out at the city from the upper deck of an open-top bus. We were given headphones and were able to listen to all the interesting commentary about the places that we saw on each stop. My plan was to ride the bus around one loop and then from there I could see where I wanted to stop off.

The bus went from Table Mountain to Camps Bay, a beautiful and rich suburb on the coast of the Atlantic, around to the Victoria and Albert Waterfront, through the city to District Six and up Long Street. It was a great way to hear about the history and little stories that you would never know unless you researched it. I heard about the rich lifestyles of the people who lived in Camps Bay, about the forced evacuations of District Six, and the history of the old fort and the town hall.

Once I had done a complete loop, I got off at Camp's Bay to have some lunch. Camp's Bay is magnificently located on the Atlantic Ocean, at the foot of the Twelve Apostles mountain range and adjacent to Table Mountain. It was the wealthy suburb of Cape Town. However, even at a nice restaurant there, I still had my order messed up twice and then ended up almost leaving because of the long wait for the bill, water, food, etc. I just didn't have good luck at restaurants in Africa.

Later, I made my way to District Six. After World War II, during the earlier part of the apartheid era, District Six was a multi-cultural hub and made up largely of "colored" residents which included Cape Malays, black Xhosa residents, and a smaller numbers of Afrikaans, whites, and Indians. However, residents were forced to relocate on February 11th, 1966, when the government declared District Six a whites-only area under the Group Areas Act. By 1982, more than 60,000 people had been relocated about 15 miles away. The old houses were bulldozed.

Government officials gave four primary reasons for the removals. In accordance with apartheid philosophy, it stated that "interracial interaction bred conflict, necessitating the separation of the races". They deemed District Six "a slum, fit only for clearance, not rehabilitation". They also portrayed the area as "crime-ridden and dangerous; they claimed that the district was a vice den, full of immoral activities like gambling, drinking, and prostitution". Though these were the official reasons, most residents believed that the government sought the land because of its proximity to the city center, Table Mountain, and the harbor.

International and local pressure made redevelopment difficult for the government, however. Since the fall of apartheid in 1994, the South African government has recognized the older claims of former residents to the area, and pledged to support rebuilding. It was the happy ending to a sad story and one that signaled things were changing for the better in South Africa in regards to race relations.

***

The next day I decided to just walk around the city. After the wonderful hop-on, hop-off bus, I felt like I had seen everything that I wanted to see. It was a nice day to walk around. The only place that was really left to see was Table Mountain. The previous day it had been closed due to high winds. It was possible to hike up but the staff at the hostel didn't recommend it because previously people had died by falling off steep ledges due to the high winds. I wasn't going to chance it.

However, this particular day it was open and a group of us planned to go up to see the sunset. At around 4 P.M. we met and took a taxi up to the cable car station at the foot of Table Mountain. I didn't realize that half of Cape Town and all its tourists were going to have the same idea as us and go up Table Mountain at the same time. The line was horrendous. However, we were already there so decided to stick with it. It took two hours of waiting to step foot on the cable car. The cable car was a revolving one so you could see a 360 degree view of Cape Town. And the views on the top of Table Mountain were incredible. On one side you could see endless sea, with the waves crashing onto the shore in perfect rhythm, framed by lush and towering mountains rimmed by clouds. On the other side you could see Robben Island, where Nelson Mandela was incarcerated, as well as Lion's Head Peak and the entire city skyline. It was stunning and the time that we arrived was perfect, as the sun was low in the sky and cast a golden glow on the ocean. The clouds began to move over the mountains and sea as the sun set lower in the sky. It was fantastic. I could also see why Table Mountain was called Table Mountain, because the top of it was entirely flat like a pancake. The only downside of the whole experience was the cold.

After the sunset, we headed to the line, which stretched way back, back , back...an undesirable length, really. I knew it would be at least two hours, if not another two and half to get back down the mountain. This time, however, the wind had picked up speed and was streaming over the top of the mountain with its icy current. Who knew it could be so cold in summer at the top of a mountain? After a miserable wait, we finally made it down to discover that there was no way to get back to our hostel. The buses had stopped running and there were no taxis. We finally managed to wave down a taxi driver who seemed to be the only one who had considered going to the top of Table Mountain at this hour. He sensed our desperation, that's for sure and charged us *ten times* the amount that we had been charged on the way there during the day. No matter what we said, he wouldn't change his price and it was either pay him the exorbitant fee or walk down to the hostel in unknown parts of an already dangerous city for another two hours. He won.

***

The next morning was my final day in Cape Town. My flight back to London departed in the early evening and so I had the morning and afternoon to explore what I hadn't seen so far. The area that I really wanted to go to was the colorful Cape Malay district. The Cape Malay people were actually brought to South Africa as slaves and although the name implies they have a Malaysian origin, the slaves were actually from Indonesia. While they were slaves, they were not allowed to have colorful clothes or houses so when they were free, they painted their houses in the brightest of colors. I found it to be a lovely expression of artistic freedom.

In the Cape Malay district, the houses were picture-perfect, painted in lovely shades of lilac, baby blue, blush pink, sunny yellow, and deep green. The neighborhood looked very cheerful. I decided to have Cape Malay food, a specialty of which is *bobotie*, an egg custard and minced meat dish that is baked until the egg sets on top. It's a food you can find nowhere else. The restaurant specialized in Cape Malay food and the *bobotie* was delicious, served with yellow, savory rice. I was not disappointed.

It was hard to believe that my African safari, or journey, was nearing its end. I looked around Cape Town and it seemed so different to Nairobi, where I had started off. Between here and there, I had seen some of Africa. My interpretation however, was only one reality. Africa was an intriguing place, somewhere I had never been before so naturally I had been curious about it and anxious to see it. To me, it no longer seemed like such an exotic and foreign place, but rather a place that I was now comfortable with and could look fondly upon. It wasn't the dark Africa of the news stories, of violent wars and crippling poverty. For me, fortunately, it wasn't this and I had been lucky enough to not see this part of Africa. Africa to me, was a place where people were trying to make it and survive, a place where communities were the glue of the culture, and a place where the people had hopes and dreams of a better future. Just like you and me. Africa had shown me *pole-pole*. *Slowly, slowly*. For me, this was Africa's final gift. Patience.

After lunch it was time to go back to the hostel to say my last goodbyes before leaving the continent forever. Well, perhaps not forever. The witchdoctor in Malawi promised that I would return someday. One never knew.

Review Request

If you enjoyed this book or if you found it useful I'd be very grateful if you'd post a positive review. Your support really does matter and it really does make a difference. And I do read all reviews so I can get your feedback.

If you'd like to leave a review then all you need to do is go to the review section on the book's Amazon page. You'll see a big button that says "Write a customer review"-click that and you're good to go! Thanks again for your support.

Best Regards,

Jamie

Works Consulted

Ham, Anthony. *Africa (Lonely Planet Multi Country Guides)*. Lonely Planet Publications Ltd; 12th edition edition (23 July 2010).

Theroux, Paul. *Dark Star Safari: Overland from Cairo to Capetown*. Penguin Group. 2003. First published by Hamish Hamilton 2002.

Internet Works Consulted

Map of Africa

http://www.dreamstime.com/stock-photography-map-africa-image6044052#

Mmegi Online. "The zebra, Botswana's lovable and graceful national animal." Gasebal We Seretse
http://www.mmegi.bw/index.php?sid=6&aid=7268&dir=2010/December/Friday10

The Guardian UK online "Robert Mugabe's land reform comes under fresh scrutiny" May 10th, 2013. David Smith.
http://www.guardian.co.uk/world/2013/may/10/robert-mugabe-land-reform

"Crater Lake."
http://www.africanspicesafaris.com/crater_lake_game_sanctuary_kenya.html

"Lake Buyoni and Kabale Pocket Guide."
http://edirisa.org/lakebunyonyi&kabale.pdf

"Living in Kigale"

http://www.livinginkigali.com/

"Hippos." African Wildlife Foundation.

http://web.archive.org/web/20101119172410/http://awf.or

g/content/wildlife/detail/hippopotamus

"Lions." BBC.

http://www.bbc.co.uk/nature/life/Lion

"Rock Hyrax." Outta Africa.

http://www.outtoafrica.nl/animals/enghyrax.html

"History of Cape Town"

http://www.capetown.at/heritage/

"Terrorist Attacks in Kenya." Wikipedia.

http://en.wikipedia.org/wiki/2012%E2%80%932013_

terrorist_attacks_in_Kenya

Made in the USA
Lexington, KY
05 July 2013